The Ultimate Zero Point
Weight Loss Cookbook

Super Easy & Delicious Zero Point Diet Recipes for Beginners | Time- and Energy-Saving | No-Stress 60-Day Meal Plan

Nanci Kelley

© **Copyright 2025 – All Rights Reserved.**

The content contained within this book may not be reproduced, duplicated or transmitted without direct written permission from the author or the publisher.

Under no circumstances will any blame or legal responsibility be held against the publisher, or author, for any damages, reparation, or monetary loss due to the information contained within this book, either directly or indirectly.

Legal Notice:

This book is copyright protected. It is only for personal use. You cannot amend, distribute, sell, use, quote or paraphrase any part, or the content within this book, without the consent of the author or publisher.

Disclaimer Notice:

Please note the information contained within this document is for educational and entertainment purposes only. All effort has been executed to present accurate, up to date, reliable, complete information. No warranties of any kind are declared or implied. Readers acknowledge that the author is not engaged in the rendering of legal, financial, medical or professional advice. The content within this book has been derived from various sources. Please consult a licensed professional before attempting any techniques outlined in this book.

By reading this document, the reader agrees that under no circumstances is the author responsible for any losses, direct or indirect, that are incurred as a result of the use of the information contained within this document, including, but not limited to, errors, omissions, or inaccuracies.

Table of Contents

- **1** Introduction
- **2** The Fundamentals of Zero Point Weight Loss
- **21** 8-Week Meal Plan
- **25** Chapter 1 Breakfast Recipes
- **33** Chapter 2 Vegetable and Side Recipes
- **40** Chapter 3 Grain and Bean Recipes
- **48** Chapter 4 Snack and Appetizer Recipes
- **55** Chapter 5 Poultry Recipes
- **64** Chapter 6 Beef, Pork, and Lamb Recipes
- **73** Chapter 7 Fish and Seafood Recipes
- **82** Chapter 8 Soup and Stew Recipes
- **89** Chapter 9 Salad Recipes
- **98** Conclusion
- **99** Appendix 1 Measurement Conversion Chart
- **100** Appendix 2 Recipes Index

Introduction

In the ever-changing landscape of healthy eating and weight management, finding a sustainable approach can feel overwhelming. There are endless diets, food plans, and strategies to choose from, and it's easy to feel lost in the sea of options. That's where The Ultimate Zero Point Weight Loss Cookbook steps in, offering a simple yet effective solution. Zero point foods are not only the foundation of a balanced diet but also a game-changer in your journey toward a healthier lifestyle. These foods allow you to indulge in wholesome, flavorful meals without constantly worrying about overindulging.

This cookbook is designed to empower you to create satisfying, delicious dishes that fit seamlessly into your weight-loss goals. Whether you're a seasoned home cook or someone just starting to explore the kitchen, this collection of recipes is accessible, inspiring, and adaptable. Each recipe focuses on nutrient-dense, zero point ingredients that support your well-being without compromising on taste.

From hearty breakfasts that energize your day to vibrant salads, comforting soups, and even indulgent desserts, this cookbook proves that healthy eating doesn't have to be boring or restrictive. You'll discover how easy it is to create meals that satisfy your hunger and nourish your body without the stress of counting every calorie.

With the help of The Ultimate Zero Point Weight Loss Cookbook, you'll learn to approach food in a whole new way—one that's sustainable, enjoyable, and free from guilt. Say goodbye to bland, uninspiring "diet" food and hello to meals bursting with flavor and vitality. Get ready to embark on a culinary journey that makes eating well feel effortless, exciting, and rewarding. Let these recipes inspire you to take control of your health and enjoy every step of the process.

The Fundamentals of Zero Point Weight Loss

Zero point weight loss revolves around the concept of eating certain foods freely without tracking or measuring, as they are low in calories, high in nutrients, and naturally satisfying. This approach provides a flexible and sustainable way to lose weight without the stress of constantly counting points or calories. By incorporating Zero point foods into your daily meals, you can enjoy the freedom of eating generously while staying on track. This method is not about deprivation; it's about empowering you to make healthier, mindful choices that promote long-term success.

Zero point foods focus on promoting fullness, balancing blood sugar levels, and supporting overall health. They include lean proteins, non-starchy vegetables, and other nutrient-dense options that provide a foundation for wholesome meals. By embracing these foods, you'll learn to listen to your body's hunger cues, enjoy more flavorful dishes, and establish habits that sustain your goals over time.

What is Zero Point Foods?

Zero point foods are the backbone of a flexible weight-loss plan. These are foods you can eat freely without tracking, thanks to their low-calorie, high-nutrient profiles. They include lean proteins like chicken breast, turkey, and eggs, as well as non-starchy vegetables, fruits, and plain nonfat yogurt. These foods are chosen for their ability to promote satiety, stabilize energy levels, and minimize cravings. By incorporating Zero point foods into your meals, you create a foundation for balanced, satisfying eating.

Zero point foods aren't just about weight loss—they also support overall health by delivering essential vitamins, minerals, and fiber. Whether you're making a quick snack or a hearty dinner, these foods provide endless options to keep your meals exciting and delicious.

The Science Behind Zero Point Foods

The effectiveness of Zero point foods lies in their impact on satiety and metabolism. Foods high in water content, fiber, and lean protein tend to keep you fuller for longer while delivering fewer calories. For instance, non-starchy vegetables are nutrient-dense but low in energy, which means you can enjoy large portions without consuming excessive calories. Proteins like eggs and fish boost metabolism and reduce hunger hormones, making them excellent staples for weight management.

This approach aligns with the principles of volumetrics, which emphasize the importance of food volume in controlling hunger. By focusing on Zero point foods, you'll naturally reduce your calorie intake while maintaining a balanced, satisfying diet. This science-backed method helps you lose weight sustainably without the mental burden of constant calorie counting.

Benefits of a Zero Point Approach

The Zero point approach is more than just a weight-loss strategy—it's a lifestyle change that simplifies your journey to better health. Here are the benefits of Zero Point Approach:

Simplifies Meal Planning and Tracking: Reduces the stress of measuring and counting calories or points for certain foods. Allows more flexibility and freedom in your daily meal choices.

Encourages Healthier Eating Habits: Promotes the consumption of nutrient-dense, whole foods. Reduces reliance on processed and high-calorie foods.

Supports Sustainable Weight Loss: Makes it easier to maintain a calorie deficit without feeling deprived. Helps build long-term habits for a healthy lifestyle.

Enhances Satiety and Reduces Cravings: Zero point foods, such as lean proteins and fiber-rich vegetables, keep you fuller for longer. Reduces the likelihood of snacking on unhealthy options.

Increases Flexibility for Social Events and Dining Out: Provides a framework to make smart choices without feeling restricted. Allows you to enjoy meals with family and friends while staying on track.

Boosts Overall Health: Improves digestion, energy levels, and nutrient intake. Supports a balanced diet that contributes to long-term well-being.

By embracing the Zero point approach, you unlock the potential to eat well, feel great, and achieve your goals with ease and confidence.

Comprehensive Zero Point Food List

Zero point foods are the cornerstone of a sustainable and flexible weight-loss plan. These foods are naturally low in calories, nutrient-dense, and designed to keep you feeling full and satisfied. They provide endless possibilities for creating healthy and delicious meals without the need for constant tracking or measuring. Below is a detailed list of Zero point foods, categorized to help you easily incorporate them into your daily routine.

1. Lean Proteins

High in protein and low in fat, these foods support muscle growth and keep you feeling fuller for longer.

Skinless chicken breast
Skinless turkey breast
Egg whites
Tofu (firm or silken)
Tempeh
Edamame
Plain, nonfat Greek yogurt
Nonfat cottage cheese
Shrimp
Lobster
Scallops
Crab
White fish (e.g., cod, tilapia, haddock)

2. Non-Starchy Vegetables

Rich in fiber, vitamins, and minerals, these vegetables can be eaten in unlimited quantities.

Leafy greens (spinach, kale, lettuce)
Broccoli
Cauliflower
Zucchini
Bell peppers
Carrots
Cucumbers
Tomatoes
Green beans
Mushrooms
Eggplant
Cabbage
Asparagus
Radishes
Brussels sprouts
Onions
Leeks
Celery

3. Fruits
Packed with natural sweetness and essential nutrients, fruits are a satisfying Zero point snack.
Apples
Bananas
Berries (strawberries, blueberries, raspberries, blackberries)
Oranges
Grapes
Watermelon
Pineapple
Mango
Kiwi
Peaches
Plums
Cherries
Papaya
Pears

4. Legumes and Beans
These are excellent plant-based protein sources that also provide fiber and essential nutrients.
Black beans
Chickpeas
Lentils
Kidney beans
Pinto beans
Cannellini beans

Split peas
Mung beans

5. Seafood
A lean protein source rich in omega-3 fatty acids and other essential nutrients.
Salmon (fresh or canned in water)
Tuna (fresh or canned in water)
Cod
Tilapia
Halibut
Clams
Mussels

6. Herbs and Spices
These add flavor and variety to your meals without adding points.
Basil
Cilantro
Parsley
Dill
Mint
Thyme
Rosemary
Garlic
Ginger
Turmeric
Paprika
Chili powder
Oregano
Cumin
Black pepper

7. Beverages
Stay hydrated with these Zero point drink options.
Water (plain, sparkling, or infused with fruits)
Unsweetened tea (green, black, herbal)
Black coffee (without sugar or cream)

8. Condiments and Flavor Enhancers
These can enhance your dishes without adding unnecessary calories.
Mustard
Vinegar (balsamic, apple cider, white, rice)
Salsa (without added sugar)
Hot sauce
Lemon and lime juice
Soy sauce (low-sodium, in moderation)

9. Soups and Broths
Use these as a base for hearty, Zero point meals.
Vegetable broth (low-sodium)
Chicken broth (low-sodium)
Miso soup (made with low-sodium miso paste)

This comprehensive Zero point food list gives you the freedom to create a wide variety of meals that are both delicious and aligned with your health goals. By incorporating these foods into your daily diet, you'll enjoy satisfying meals, stay on track, and build a healthy, balanced lifestyle. Let this list be your guide as you explore new flavors, experiment with recipes, and make Zero point eating a seamless part of your journey!

Building Your Zero Point Kitchen

Creating a Zero point kitchen is essential for long-term success. By stocking your pantry with the right staples and equipping your kitchen with useful tools, you'll be ready to whip up delicious, healthy meals in no time. A well-organized kitchen saves time, reduces stress, and helps you stay consistent with your weight-loss goals. And here are how to build your zero kitchen:

Stock Essential Pantry Staples:
1. Canned beans, lentils, and chickpeas.
2. Low-sodium broths, whole grains like quinoa and brown rice.
3. Spices, dried herbs, and vinegar for flavoring.

Include Fresh and Frozen Ingredients:
1. Fresh fruits, non-starchy vegetables, and leafy greens.
2. Frozen vegetables and fruits for quick, healthy meals.

Keep Lean Proteins on Hand:
1. Skinless chicken breast, turkey, eggs, and fish.
2. Non-fat plain Greek yogurt and cottage cheese.

Equip Your Kitchen with Must-Have Tools:
1. Good-quality knife, cutting board, and non-stick pans.
2. Slow cooker, food processor, and mixing bowls for efficient meal prep.

Organize Your Kitchen for Easy Access:
1. Use clear containers for prepped ingredients and leftovers.
2. Label and date stored foods to ensure freshness and reduce waste.

With your Zero point kitchen in place, you'll feel empowered to create delicious, health-focused meals that align with your goals every single day.

Smart Meal Planning with Zero Points

Smart meal planning is a powerful tool that transforms healthy eating from a daunting task into an achievable and enjoyable routine. Here are about Smart Meal Planning with Zero Points:

Plan a Weekly Menu:
1. Choose a variety of Zero point foods to build balanced meals for the week.
2. Include options for breakfast, lunch, dinner, and snacks.

Prep Meals in Advance:
1. Batch cook soups, stews, and roasted vegetables for easy reheating.

2. Store prepped ingredients in portioned containers for grab-and-go meals.

Focus on Balance and Variety:
1. Combine lean proteins, vegetables, and fruits to create satisfying meals.
2. Incorporate herbs, spices, and citrus to keep flavors exciting.

Batch Cook and Freeze:
1. Prepare large portions of your favorite Zero point meals and freeze extras.
2. Use freezer-safe containers to ensure freshness and convenience.

Adapt for Dining Out and Busy Days:
1. Plan for meals at restaurants by choosing Zero point friendly dishes in advance.
2. Keep simple Zero point snacks, like boiled eggs or fruit, ready for busy days.

By mastering the art of meal planning, you pave the way for a smoother, healthier lifestyle where delicious Zero point meals are always within reach.

Staying Motivated on Your Journey

Staying motivated throughout your weight-loss journey is essential for achieving long-term success. While initial enthusiasm can drive early progress, maintaining that momentum requires consistent effort, strategic planning, and the ability to adapt to challenges. By tracking progress, overcoming plateaus, and celebrating non-scale victories, you'll build a solid foundation to keep moving forward with confidence and determination.

Tracking Progress

Tracking your progress is a powerful way to stay motivated and accountable. It allows you to measure both your successes and areas for improvement, giving you a clear picture of how far you've come.

1. Use a Food Journal or App
Record everything you eat, including portion sizes and calorie counts, to stay mindful of your choices. Reflect on your eating patterns to identify what works best for your body.

2. Track Physical Activity
Log your workouts, steps, or active minutes to monitor improvements in your fitness levels. Use fitness trackers or apps to set daily or weekly activity goals.

3. Document Body Measurements
Measure your waist, hips, arms, and thighs regularly to track physical changes. Take progress photos to visually see the transformation over time.

4. Monitor Your Weight Thoughtfully
Weigh yourself consistently but not obsessively—once a week at the same time of day is ideal. Focus on long-term trends rather than daily fluctuations, which can be influenced by water retention or other factors.

Consistently tracking your progress keeps you motivated by providing tangible evidence of your efforts. It allows you to celebrate your wins and make informed adjustments to stay on course.

Overcoming Plateaus

Weight-loss plateaus are a common challenge, but they're not a sign of failure. Overcoming these hurdles requires understanding your body's adaptations and making strategic changes to reignite progress.

1. Reevaluate Your Calorie Intake
As you lose weight, your body's energy needs decrease. Adjust your portion sizes and daily calorie targets accordingly. Focus on nutrient-dense, low-calorie foods like leafy greens, lean proteins, and whole grains.

2. Revamp Your Exercise Routine
Introduce new activities or increase the intensity of your workouts to challenge your body in different ways. Incorporate strength training to build muscle, which boosts metabolism and helps break through plateaus.

3. Prioritize Hydration and Sleep
Drink plenty of water to support metabolism and reduce bloating. Ensure you're getting 7-9 hours of quality sleep per night to regulate hunger hormones and improve recovery.

4. Practice Patience and Persistence
Remember that plateaus are a natural part of the process. Stay consistent with your healthy habits, and progress will resume. Use this time to focus on building sustainable habits rather than quick fixes.

Plateaus are opportunities to reassess and refine your approach. By staying adaptable and consistent, you'll overcome these challenges and continue moving toward your goals.

The Importance of Non-Scale Victories

Weight loss is about more than just the number on the scale. Non-scale victories (NSVs) highlight the many ways your health and well-being are improving, keeping you motivated and focused on the bigger picture.

1. Improved Energy and Stamina
Notice how everyday tasks, like climbing stairs or running errands, feel easier and more manageable. Celebrate newfound energy that allows you to engage in activities you once found tiring.

2. Enhanced Fitness and Strength
Track improvements in your workouts, such as running longer distances, lifting heavier weights, or mastering a challenging yoga pose. Recognize milestones, like completing a race or achieving a personal fitness goal.

3. Clothing Fits Better
Enjoy the moment when you fit into a smaller size or rediscover clothes that had been tucked away in your closet. Use these changes as visual and tangible proof of your progress.

4. Boosted Confidence and Mood
Relish the increased self-esteem and pride that comes with taking control of your health. Notice a positive shift in your mental and emotional well-being, such as reduced stress and greater happiness.

5. Health Benefits Beyond Weight
Celebrate improvements in blood pressure, cholesterol levels, or reduced joint pain. Feel proud of taking steps that reduce your risk of chronic diseases and improve your quality of life. Non-scale victories remind you that success is more than a number. By recognizing and celebrating these achievements, you'll stay motivated and committed to your journey, appreciating the many ways your life is transforming for the better.

Motivation is a critical driver of success, and maintaining it requires thoughtful strategies. By tracking progress, overcoming plateaus, and celebrating non-scale victories, you'll stay energized and inspired on your journey. Embrace every milestone, big or small, and continue building the healthy, fulfilling lifestyle you deserve.

Five Exclusive Bonuses

Take your Zero point journey to the next level with these Five Exclusive Bonuses! Each bonus is thoughtfully designed to enhance your experience, offering practical tips, creative recipes, and global inspiration to keep your meals exciting, healthy, and delicious. From mastering Zero Point Food Swaps to crafting festive dishes with Zero Point Holiday Recipes, exploring diverse flavors with Global Zero Point Cuisine, elevating your meals with Zero Point Sauces and Dressings, and embracing plant-based options with Plant-Based Zero Point Recipes, these bonuses provide everything you need to stay on track and love every bite.

Zero Point Food Swaps
Making smart food swaps is a simple yet effective way to enjoy your favorite dishes while staying aligned with your weight-loss goals. Zero point food swaps allow you to cut calories without sacrificing flavor or satisfaction, empowering you to make healthier choices every day. Here are smart substitutions for everyday ingredients and how to transform high-calorie recipes into zero point favorites:

Smart Substitutions for Everyday Ingredients:

1. Swap High-Calorie Carbohydrates for Zero Point Alternatives
Replace pasta with spiralized zucchini or spaghetti squash for a low-calorie, nutrient-dense alternative. Use cauliflower rice instead of white or brown rice in stir-fries, casseroles, or side dishes.

2. Replace High-Fat Proteins with Lean Options
Substitute ground beef with ground turkey or chicken in tacos, burgers, and meatballs. Choose skinless chicken breast, fish, or plant-based proteins like tofu over higher-fat cuts of meat.

3. Use Zero Point Dairy Alternatives
Replace heavy cream or full-fat milk with unsweetened almond milk, skim milk, or nonfat plain Greek yogurt in recipes. Swap sour cream

for nonfat plain yogurt in dips, dressings, and baked dishes.

4. Opt for Flavor Enhancers Without the Extra Points

Use herbs, spices, garlic, and citrus juice to season dishes instead of butter, oil, or high-sodium sauces. Replace mayonnaise with mashed avocado or mustard for spreads and dressings.

5. Switch to Zero Point Sweeteners

Replace sugar with natural zero-calorie sweeteners like stevia or monk fruit in baking and beverages. Use mashed bananas or unsweetened applesauce to add natural sweetness to baked goods.

Incorporating Zero point food swaps into your routine makes it easy to enjoy the foods you love while staying on track. These substitutions not only reduce calories but also boost the nutritional value of your meals, helping you build a healthier lifestyle.

Transforming High-Calorie Recipes into Zero Point Favorites

Transforming your favorite high-calorie recipes into Zero point versions is a fun and rewarding way to stay committed to your goals without feeling deprived. With a few creative tweaks and Zero point substitutions, you can recreate comforting, satisfying meals that align with your weight-loss plan.

1. Reinventing Creamy Soups and Sauces

Replace heavy cream with blended cauliflower or nonfat Greek yogurt to create rich, creamy textures without added calories. Use low-sodium vegetable or chicken broth as a base for soups instead of high-fat options.

2. Lightening Up Casseroles and Bakes

Substitute cheese with reduced-fat or plant-based cheese alternatives, or use nutritional yeast for a cheesy flavor. Replace starchy bases like potatoes or pasta with layers of zucchini, eggplant, or spaghetti squash.

3. Zero point Desserts

Use blended frozen bananas or nonfat Greek yogurt as a base for homemade ice cream. Replace flour with oat flour or almond meal and sweeten baked goods with fruit purees or zero-calorie sweeteners.

4. Revamping Fried Foods

Swap deep frying for air frying or baking to achieve crispy textures with less fat. Coat proteins or vegetables with whole-wheat breadcrumbs or crushed cornflakes instead of batter.

5. Turning Takeout Favorites into Zero Point Meals

Recreate dishes like fried rice or lo mein using cauliflower rice and stir-fried vegetables. Make pizza using a base of eggplant or a thin whole-grain tortilla topped with Zero point ingredients.

Transforming high-calorie recipes into Zero point favorites allows you to indulge in your favorite meals guilt-free. With these simple adjustments, you'll enjoy delicious, satisfying dishes that support your goals and make healthy eating feel like second nature.

Zero Point Holiday Recipes

The holidays are a time for celebration, but they can also present challenges when trying to maintain a healthy eating plan. With Zero Point Holiday Recipes, you can enjoy all the festivities while staying on track. From flavorful appetizers to indulgent yet guilt-free desserts, these recipes ensure you'll feel satisfied and proud of your choices during the season.

1. Festive Appetizers

Stuffed Mini Bell Peppers

Ingredients:
10 mini bell peppers
1 cup nonfat Greek yogurt
2 cloves garlic, minced
2 tbsp fresh parsley, chopped
1 tsp paprika

Steps:
1. Slice the mini bell peppers in half and remove the seeds. 2. In a bowl, mix the Greek yogurt, garlic, parsley, and paprika. 3. Fill each pepper half with the yogurt mixture. 4. Serve chilled on a festive platter.

Shrimp Cocktail

Ingredients:
1 lb cooked shrimp, peeled and deveined
½ cup sugar-free ketchup
2 tbsp prepared horseradish
Juice of 1 lemon

Steps:
1. Mix the ketchup, horseradish, and lemon juice in a small bowl to make the cocktail sauce. 2. Arrange the shrimp on a platter with the sauce in the center. 3. Garnish with the lemon wedges and parsley.

2. Main Courses for Special Occasions

Herb-Crusted Turkey Breast

Ingredients:
1 turkey breast (about 2 lbs)
3 tbsp fresh rosemary, chopped
2 tbsp fresh thyme, chopped
3 cloves garlic, minced
Zest of 1 lemon

Steps:
1. Preheat the oven to 375°F (190°C). 2. Mix the rosemary, thyme, garlic, and lemon zest in a bowl. 3. Rub the herb mixture all over the turkey breast. 4. Place the turkey in a roasting pan and roast for 1½ hours or until internal temperature reaches 165°F (74°C).

Salmon with Dill and Lemon

Ingredients:
4 salmon fillets
1 lemon, sliced
2 tbsp fresh dill, chopped
Salt and black pepper to taste

Steps:
1. Preheat the oven to 400°F (200°C). 2. Place the salmon fillets on a baking sheet lined with parchment paper. 3. Top each fillet with the lemon slices and sprinkle with dill, salt, and pepper. 4. Bake for 12-15 minutes until the salmon flakes easily with a fork.

3. Guilt-Free Holiday Desserts

Baked Cinnamon Apples

Ingredients:
4 medium apples
1 tsp ground cinnamon

¼ tsp nutmeg
2 tbsp sugar-free maple syrup

Steps:
1. Preheat the oven to 350°F (175°C). 2. Core the apples and place them in a baking dish. 3. Mix the cinnamon, nutmeg, and maple syrup, then drizzle over the apples. 4. Bake for 30-35 minutes or until tender.

Berry Parfaits

Ingredients:
2 cups mixed berries (strawberries, blueberries, raspberries)
1½ cups nonfat Greek yogurt
1 tsp vanilla extract

Steps:
1. In a bowl, mix the Greek yogurt with vanilla extract. 2. Layer the berries and yogurt in a serving glasses, starting with the yogurt. 3. Repeat the layers until the glasses are filled. 4. Chill before serving.

With these festive recipes, your holiday meals can be both delicious and health-conscious. From appetizers to desserts, you'll enjoy the season without straying from your goals.

Global Zero Point Cuisine

Take your taste buds on a global journey with these Zero point recipes inspired by Mediterranean, Asian, and Latin American cuisines. These simple yet flavorful dishes will add excitement to your meals while helping you stay on track.

1. Mediterranean-Inspired Dishes

Greek Salad with Lemon Dressing

Ingredients:
1 cucumber, diced
2 tomatoes, diced
1 red onion, thinly sliced
¼ cup fresh parsley, chopped
Juice of 1 lemon
1 tsp oregano

Steps:
1. Combine the cucumber, tomatoes, red onion, and parsley in a bowl. 2. In a small bowl, whisk the lemon juice and oregano. 3. Pour the dressing over the salad, toss, and serve.

Mediterranean Lentil Soup

Ingredients:
1 cup dry lentils
1 onion, chopped
2 carrots, sliced
4 cups vegetable broth
1 tsp cumin

Steps:
1. In a pot, sauté the onion and carrots until soft. 2. Add the lentils, broth, and cumin. 3. Simmer for 25-30 minutes until the lentils are tender.

2. Asian-Inspired Flavors

Stir-Fried Vegetables

Ingredients:
1 cup broccoli florets
1 cup snap peas
1 carrot, julienned
2 cloves garlic, minced
1 tbsp soy sauce

Steps:
1. Heat a non-stick pan and sauté garlic until fragrant. 2. Add the vegetables and stir-fry for 5-7 minutes. 3. Drizzle the soy sauce over and toss before serving.

Miso Soup

Ingredients:
4 cups water
2 tbsp miso paste
½ cup tofu, cubed
1 sheet seaweed, chopped
2 green onions, sliced

Steps:
1. Bring water to a boil, then reduce to a simmer. 2. Stir in the miso paste until dissolved. 3. Add the tofu, seaweed, and green onions, and simmer for 5 minutes.

3. Latin American Zero Point Recipes

Black Bean and Corn Salad

Ingredients:
1 can black beans, rinsed
1 cup corn kernels
1 red bell pepper, diced
Juice of 1 lime
¼ cup cilantro, chopped

Steps:
1. Combine the black beans, corn, and bell pepper in a bowl. 2. Drizzle the lime juice over the salad and mix well. 3. Garnish with the cilantro and serve.

Grilled Fish Tacos

Ingredients:
4 small corn tortillas
2 white fish fillets
1 cup shredded cabbage
¼ cup salsa
1 lime, sliced

Steps:
1. Grill the fish fillets until cooked through. 2. Warm the tortillas and fill each with fish, cabbage, and salsa. 3. Squeeze the lime juice over before serving.

These global recipes bring bold flavors to your kitchen while supporting your health goals. From the Mediterranean to Asia and Latin America, enjoy the culinary adventure guilt-free!

Zero Point Sauces and Dressings

The right sauce or dressing can elevate any dish, transforming simple ingredients into something extraordinary. With Zero Point Sauces and Dressings, you'll learn to create flavorful marinades, creamy dressings, and savory sauces that enhance your meals while keeping them healthy and light. These recipes are quick, versatile, and perfect for adding zest to your favorite dishes.

1. Flavorful Marinades

Lemon Herb Marinade

Ingredients:
Juice of 2 lemons
3 tbsp fresh parsley, chopped
2 tbsp fresh thyme, chopped
3 garlic cloves, minced
1 tsp black pepper

Steps:
1. Combine all ingredients in a bowl and whisk together. 2. Pour over the chicken, fish, or tofu, and marinate for at least 30 minutes. 3. Cook as desired (grill, bake, or pan-sear).

Soy Ginger Marinade

Ingredients:
¼ cup soy sauce (low-sodium)
2 tbsp rice vinegar
1 tbsp fresh ginger, grated
2 garlic cloves, minced
½ tsp chili flakes (optional)

Steps:

1. Mix all ingredients in a bowl. 2. Marinate your choice of protein or vegetables for 20-30 minutes. 3. Cook to your preference and enjoy bold, Asian-inspired flavors.

2. Creamy Guilt-Free Salad Dressings

Greek Yogurt Ranch Dressing

Ingredients:

1 cup nonfat Greek yogurt
1 tbsp fresh dill, chopped
1 tbsp fresh chives, chopped
1 tsp garlic powder
1 tsp onion powder
2 tbsp lemon juice

Steps:

1. In a small bowl, whisk together the Greek yogurt, dill, chives, garlic powder, onion powder, and lemon juice. 2. Chill for 15 minutes before serving over the salads or as a dip for veggies.

Avocado Lime Dressing

Ingredients:

1 ripe avocado
Juice of 1 lime
¼ cup fresh cilantro
¼ cup water
1 garlic clove, minced

Steps:

1. Blend all ingredients in a food processor until smooth. 2. Adjust water for desired consistency. 3. Drizzle over the salads or use as a topping for tacos.

3. Savory Zero Point Sauces

Tomato Basil Sauce

Ingredients:

1 can (14 oz) crushed tomatoes (no salt added)
2 garlic cloves, minced
¼ cup fresh basil, chopped
1 tsp oregano
Salt and pepper to taste

Steps:

1. In a saucepan, sauté the garlic until fragrant. 2. Add the crushed tomatoes, oregano, and basil. 3. Simmer for 15-20 minutes. Serve over the pasta, zoodles, or grilled proteins.

Mushroom Gravy

Ingredients:

1 cup mushrooms, finely chopped
1 cup vegetable broth (low-sodium)
1 tbsp cornstarch mixed with 2 tbsp water
½ tsp thyme

Steps:

1. Sauté the mushrooms in a non-stick pan until soft. 2. Add the vegetable broth and thyme, then bring to a boil. 3. Stir in the cornstarch mixture and simmer until thickened. Serve over the roasted vegetables or meat.

Garlic Lemon Sauce

Ingredients:

Juice of 1 lemon
3 garlic cloves, minced
¼ cup vegetable broth
1 tsp black pepper

Steps:

1. Heat a non-stick pan and sauté garlic until lightly golden. 2. Add the lemon juice, vegetable broth, and pepper. 3. Simmer for 5-7 minutes. Drizzle over the grilled fish or steamed vegetables.

Tzatziki Sauce

Ingredients:

1 cup nonfat plain Greek yogurt
1 medium cucumber, grated and squeezed to remove excess water
2 cloves garlic, minced
1 tbsp fresh dill, chopped
1 tbsp fresh lemon juice
¼ tsp salt
¼ tsp black pepper

Steps:

1. Grate the cucumber using a box grater and place it in a clean kitchen towel or paper towel. Squeeze out as much water as possible to prevent the sauce from becoming watery. 2. In a mixing bowl, combine the Greek yogurt, grated cucumber, minced garlic, and chopped dill. 3. Stir in the lemon juice, salt, and black pepper. Mix well until all ingredients are fully incorporated. 4. Cover and chill in the refrigerator for at least 30 minutes to allow the flavors to meld. 5. Serve as a dip for fresh veggies, or a topping for grilled meats.

With these Zero Point Sauces and Dressings, you can add depth and flavor to your meals without worrying about extra calories. These simple, delicious recipes will make every bite more enjoyable while keeping you on track with your health goals. Get creative, experiment with flavors, and let your cooking shine!

Plant-Based Zero Point Recipes

Plant-based eating has never been easier or more delicious. Whether you're fully vegan or simply incorporating more plant-based meals into your routine, Plant-Based Zero Point Recipes will help you stay on track without sacrificing flavor or nutrition. From protein-packed vegan options to innovative ways to cook with tofu and tempeh, and dairy-free alternatives, these recipes are designed to nourish your body and excite your taste buds.

1. High-Protein Vegan Options

Lentil and Vegetable Stew

Ingredients:
1 cup dry lentils, rinsed
1 onion, chopped
2 carrots, diced
2 celery stalks, sliced
4 cups vegetable broth
1 tsp thyme
1 bay leaf

Steps:
1. In a large pot, sauté the onion, carrots, and celery until softened. 2. Add the lentils, vegetable broth, thyme, and bay leaf. 3. Simmer for 25-30 minutes until the lentils are tender. 4. Remove the bay leaf and serve hot.

Chickpea and Spinach Stir-Fry

Ingredients:
1 can chickpeas, rinsed and drained
4 cups fresh spinach
2 garlic cloves, minced
1 tsp cumin
Juice of 1 lemon

Steps:
1. Heat a non-stick pan and sauté garlic until fragrant. 2. Add the chickpeas and cumin, stirring for 3-4 minutes. 3. Toss in the spinach and cook until wilted. 4. Drizzle with the lemon juice and serve.

2. Creative Uses for Tofu and Tempeh

Crispy Baked Tofu

Ingredients:
1 block firm tofu, pressed and cubed
2 tbsp soy sauce (low-sodium)
1 tsp garlic powder
1 tsp smoked paprika

Steps:
1. Preheat oven to 400°F (200°C). 2. Toss tofu cubes with the soy sauce, garlic powder, and smoked paprika. 3. Spread the tofu on a baking sheet lined with parchment paper. 4. Bake for 25-30 minutes, flipping halfway through, until crispy.

Teriyaki Tempeh Stir-Fry

Ingredients:
1 block tempeh, sliced thinly
¼ cup soy sauce (low-sodium)
1 tbsp rice vinegar
1 tsp ginger, grated
4 cups mixed vegetables (e.g., broccoli, bell peppers, snap peas)

Steps:
1. In a small bowl, mix the soy sauce, rice vinegar, and ginger. 2. Marinate the tempeh slices in the mixture for 15 minutes. 3. Sauté tempeh in a non-stick pan until browned. 4. Add mixed vegetables and cook until tender-crisp. Serve warm.

3. Delicious Dairy-Free Alternatives

Cashew Cream

Ingredients:

1 cup raw cashews, soaked overnight
½ cup water
Juice of ½ lemon
1 garlic clove (optional)

Steps:

1. Drain and rinse the soaked cashews. 2. Blend the cashews with water, lemon juice, and garlic until smooth. 3. Use as a dairy-free substitute for cream in soups, sauces, or pasta.

Almond Milk Cheese Spread

Ingredients:

1 cup unsweetened almond milk
2 tbsp nutritional yeast
1 tbsp cornstarch mixed with 2 tbsp water
½ tsp garlic powder

Steps:

1. Heat the almond milk in a saucepan until it starts to simmer. 2. Stir in the nutritional yeast and garlic powder. 3. Add the cornstarch mixture and whisk until thickened. 4. Use as a spread for crackers or a dip for vegetables.

With these Plant-Based Zero Point Recipes, you can enjoy satisfying, nutritious meals without adding extra points. From hearty stews and creative tofu dishes to creamy, dairy-free alternatives, these recipes make plant-based eating simple, delicious, and exciting. Dive in, explore new flavors, and feel great about every bite!

These Five Exclusive Bonuses empower you to explore a world of culinary possibilities while staying true to your goals. Whether you're making smart substitutions, preparing holiday favorites, enjoying international dishes, enhancing flavors with sauces and dressings, or diving into plant-based creations, each bonus enriches your journey with inspiration and variety. Embrace these tools to fuel your success, expand your skills, and savor the benefits of healthy, Zero point living. Your path to a healthier, more vibrant lifestyle starts here—get ready to cook, explore, and thrive!

8-Week Meal Plan

Week 1

Day 1:
Breakfast: Scrambled Eggs with Arugula and Radish Salad
Lunch: Caramelized Onion Lentil and Rice Bowl
Snack: Marinated Mushrooms and Olives
Dinner: Grilled Lemon Herb Chicken Breasts

Day 2:
Breakfast: Spinach and Mushroom Omelet
Lunch: Moroccan Lentil Soup
Snack: Air-Fried Garlic Dill Beets
Dinner: Lemon Baked Halibut with Cherry Tomatoes

Day 3:
Breakfast: Zucchini and Bell Pepper Frittata
Lunch: Sicilian Escarole and White Beans
Snack: Spiced Roasted Cashews
Dinner: Moroccan Chicken and Vegetable Tagine

Day 4:
Breakfast: Oatmeal with Apples and Cinnamon
Lunch: Lemony Quinoa with Broccoli and Potatoes
Snack: Roasted Red Pepper Tapenade
Dinner: Mediterranean Pork Chops with Olives

Day 5:
Breakfast: Cottage Cheese Breakfast Bowl
Lunch: Authentic Moussaka
Snack: Roasted Spiced Chickpeas
Dinner: Braised Lamb Shanks in Herbed Tomato Sauce

Day 6:
Breakfast: Strawberry Spinach Avocado Smoothie
Lunch: Mushroom Barley Pilaf
Snack: Lemon Garlic Shrimp
Dinner: Roasted Chicken with Tzatziki Sauce

Day 7:
Breakfast: Herbed Scrambled Eggs
Lunch: Green Bean Salad with Cilantro Sauce
Snack: Deviled Eggs with Yogurt and Dill
Dinner: Roasted Sea Bass with Root Vegetables

Week 2

Day 1:
Breakfast: Vegan Tofu Scramble
Lunch: Spiced Lentil and Butternut Squash Salad
Snack: Lemon Garlic Hummus
Dinner: Roasted Whole Red Snapper with Dill

Day 2:
Breakfast: Huevos Rancheros
Lunch: Slow Cooker Vegan Bean Chili
Snack: Marinated Mushrooms and Olives
Dinner: Braised Beef Brisket with Onions

Day 3:
Breakfast: Greek Yogurt and Berry Bowl
Lunch: Mushroom Barley Pilaf
Snack: Herbed Garlic Popcorn
Dinner: Lemon Garlic Chicken Thighs

Day 4:
Breakfast: Fried Eggs and Lettuce
Lunch: Moroccan Tomato and Roasted Pepper Salad
Snack: Sweet Potato Chips
Dinner: Grilled Spiced Pork Tenderloin

Day 5:
Breakfast: Blueberry Power Breakfast Smoothie
Lunch: Roasted Grape Tomatoes and Asparagus
Snack: Garlic Roasted Tomatoes and Olives
Dinner: Chicken Shawarma with Chickpeas and Sweet Potato

Day 6:
Breakfast: Vegetable Scramble
Lunch: Lentils with Spinach and Crispy Garlic
Snack: Turkish Spiced Mixed Nuts
Dinner: Pan-Seared Sea Bass

Day 7:
Breakfast: Blackberry Quinoa Bowl
Lunch: Lemon White Bean and Kale Soup
Snack: Stuffed Cucumber Cups
Dinner: Slow Cooker Italian Beef Ragù

Week 3

Day 1:
Breakfast: Cucumber and Tomato Salad with Egg Whites
Lunch: Italian Roasted Vegetables
Snack: Spiced Roasted Cashews
Dinner: Grilled Lemon-Garlic Salmon

Day 2:
Breakfast: Spinach and Mushroom Omelet
Lunch: Tahini Barley Salad
Snack: Pumpkin Rice Patties
Dinner: Moroccan-Spiced Sea Bass

Day 3:
Breakfast: Cottage Cheese Breakfast Bowl
Lunch: Homemade Vegetable Fagioli
Snack: Lemon Garlic Hummus
Dinner: Grilled Greek-Inspired Beef Kebabs

Day 4:
Breakfast: Blueberry Chia Oatmeal
Lunch: Asparagus, Arugula, and White Bean Salad
Snack: Garlic Roasted Tomatoes and Olives
Dinner: Roasted Chicken Breasts with Ratatouille

Day 5:
Breakfast: Tofu Scramble and Roasted Potatoes
Lunch: Baked Brown Rice with Mushrooms and Edamame
Snack: Roasted Spiced Chickpeas
Dinner: Cherry Barbecue Chicken Cutlets

Day 6:
Breakfast: Strawberry Spinach Avocado Smoothie
Lunch: Spiced Lentil and Butternut Squash Salad
Snack: Air Fryer Popcorn
Dinner: Mediterranean Slow-Cooked Turkey Breast

Day 7:
Breakfast: Herbed Scrambled Eggs
Lunch: Lemony Green Beans with Red Onions
Snack: Sweet Potato Chips
Dinner: Pan-Seared Sea Bass

Week 4

Day 1:
Breakfast: Fried Eggs and Lettuce
Lunch: Green Bean Salad with Cilantro Sauce
Snack: Lemon Garlic Shrimp
Dinner: Braised Lamb Shanks in Herbed Tomato Sauce

Day 2:
Breakfast: Cucumber and Tomato Salad with Egg Whites
Lunch: Lemon and Thyme Roasted Vegetables
Snack: Crunchy Turmeric Chickpeas
Dinner: Lemon Herbed Chicken

Day 3:
Breakfast: Scrambled Eggs with Arugula and Radish Salad
Lunch: Moroccan Rice and Chickpea Bake
Snack: Garlic Roasted Tomatoes and Olives
Dinner: Grilled Spiced Pork Tenderloin

Day 4:
Breakfast: Huevos Rancheros
Lunch: Lentils with Spinach and Crispy Garlic
Snack: Herbed Garlic Popcorn
Dinner: Baked Salmon and Cherry Tomato Pockets

Day 5:
Breakfast: Zucchini and Bell Pepper Frittata
Lunch: Roasted Grape Tomatoes and Asparagus
Snack: Air-Fried Garlic Dill Beets
Dinner: Shredded Chicken Souvlaki

Day 6:
Breakfast: Blackberry Quinoa Bowl
Lunch: Spiced Roasted Mini Potatoes
Snack: Roasted Red Pepper Tapenade
Dinner: Roasted Whole Red Snapper with Dill

Day 7:
Breakfast: Blueberry Power Breakfast Smoothie
Lunch: Slow Cooker Vegan Bean Chili
Snack: Air Fryer Roasted Radishes
Dinner: Steamed Cod with Swiss Chard

Week 5

Day 1:
Breakfast: Greek Yogurt and Berry Bowl
Lunch: Sicilian Escarole and White Beans
Snack: Sweet Potato Chips
Dinner: Chicken Shawarma with Chickpeas and Sweet Potato

Day 2:
Breakfast: Cottage Cheese Breakfast Bowl
Lunch: Lemony Quinoa with Broccoli and Potatoes
Snack: Roasted Spiced Chickpeas
Dinner: Greek Turkey and Rice Skillet

Day 3:
Breakfast: Oatmeal with Apples and Cinnamon
Lunch: White Bean and Vegetable Soup
Snack: Crispy Herbed White Beans
Dinner: Moroccan Seafood Stew

Day 4:
Breakfast: Vegan Tofu Scramble
Lunch: Greek Baked Butter Beans
Snack: Garlic Roasted Tomatoes and Olives
Dinner: Mediterranean Pork Chops with Olives

Day 5:
Breakfast: Vegetable Scramble
Lunch: Garlicky Sautéed Greens
Snack: Spiced Roasted Cashews
Dinner: Grilled Lemon-Garlic Salmon

Day 6:
Breakfast: Herbed Scrambled Eggs
Lunch: Spiced Lentil and Butternut Squash Salad
Snack: Turkish Spiced Mixed Nuts
Dinner: Braised Beef Brisket with Onions

Day 7:
Breakfast: Strawberry Spinach Avocado Smoothie
Lunch: Lentils with Spinach and Crispy Garlic
Snack: Marinated Mushrooms and Olives
Dinner: Dukkah-Spiced Cod with Beet and Arugula Salad

Week 6

Day 1:
Breakfast: Spinach and Mushroom Omelet
Lunch: Moroccan Rice and Chickpea Bake
Snack: Air Fryer Popcorn
Dinner: Braised Lamb Shanks in Herbed Tomato Sauce

Day 2:
Breakfast: Zucchini and Bell Pepper Frittata
Lunch: Lemon White Bean and Kale Soup
Snack: Lemon Garlic Shrimp
Dinner: Balsamic Rosemary Pork Tenderloin

Day 3:
Breakfast: Huevos Rancheros
Lunch: Asparagus, Arugula, and White Bean Salad
Snack: Roasted Grape Tomatoes and Asparagus
Dinner: Cherry Barbecue Chicken Cutlets

Day 4:
Breakfast: Fried Eggs and Lettuce
Lunch: Homemade Vegetable Fagioli
Snack: Sweet Potato Chips
Dinner: Lemon Herb-Crusted Pork Tenderloin

Day 5:
Breakfast: Scrambled Eggs with Arugula and Radish Salad
Lunch: Garlic Roasted Zucchini with Pepper
Snack: Crunchy Turmeric Chickpeas
Dinner: Spicy Barbecued Scallops and Shrimp

Day 6:
Breakfast: Blueberry Chia Oatmeal
Lunch: Tahini Barley Salad
Snack: Roasted Cauliflower with Lemon Tahini Sauce
Dinner: Mediterranean Slow-Cooked Turkey Breast

Day 7:
Breakfast: Blackberry Quinoa Bowl
Lunch: Slow Cooker Vegan Bean Chili
Snack: Lemon and Thyme Roasted Vegetables
Dinner: Mediterranean Beef Stew

Week 7

Day 1:
Breakfast: Herbed Scrambled Eggs
Lunch: Green Bean Salad with Cilantro Sauce
Snack: Garlic Roasted Tomatoes and Olives
Dinner: Grilled Lemon Herb Chicken Breasts

Day 2:
Breakfast: Tofu Scramble and Roasted Potatoes
Lunch: Authentic Moussaka
Snack: Roasted Spiced Chickpeas
Dinner: Braised Beef Brisket with Onions

Day 3:
Breakfast: Cottage Cheese Breakfast Bowl
Lunch: Caramelized Onion Lentil and Rice Bowl
Snack: Air-Fried Garlic Dill Beets
Dinner: Hearty Paella Soup

Day 4:
Breakfast: Strawberry Spinach Avocado Smoothie
Lunch: Garlic Roasted Brussels Sprouts with Orange
Snack: Spiced Roasted Cashews
Dinner: Roasted Pork Tenderloin with Cherry-Balsamic Sauce

Day 5:
Breakfast: Vegan Tofu Scramble
Lunch: Lemon White Bean and Kale Soup
Snack: Lemon Garlic Hummus
Dinner: Lemon Garlic Chicken Thighs

Day 6:
Breakfast: Vegetable Scramble
Lunch: Lentils with Spinach and Crispy Garlic
Snack: Garlic Roasted Zucchini with Pepper
Dinner: Citrus Swordfish with Fresh Herbs

Day 7:
Breakfast: Cucumber and Tomato Salad with Egg Whites
Lunch: Sicilian Escarole and White Beans
Snack: Sweet Potato Chips
Dinner: Grilled Spiced Pork Tenderloin

Week 8

Day 1:
Breakfast: Blueberry Power Breakfast Smoothie
Lunch: Tahini Barley Salad
Snack: Roasted Red Pepper Tapenade
Dinner: Chicken Shawarma with Chickpeas and Sweet Potato

Day 2:
Breakfast: Scrambled Eggs with Arugula and Radish Salad
Lunch: Moroccan Rice and Chickpea Bake
Snack: Garlic Roasted Tomatoes and Olives
Dinner: Braised Lamb Shanks in Herbed Tomato Sauce

Day 3:
Breakfast: Oatmeal with Apples and Cinnamon
Lunch: Homemade Vegetable Fagioli
Snack: Crispy Herbed White Beans
Dinner: Grilled Lemon-Garlic Salmon

Day 4:
Breakfast: Greek Yogurt and Berry Bowl
Lunch: Oven Roasted Cauliflower with Lemon Tahini Sauce
Snack: Lemon Garlic Shrimp
Dinner: Air Fryer Herbed Tuna Steaks

Day 5:
Breakfast: Huevos Rancheros
Lunch: Spiced Lentil and Butternut Squash Salad
Snack: Stuffed Cucumber Cups
Dinner: Mediterranean Slow-Cooked Turkey Breast

Day 6:
Breakfast: Cottage Cheese Breakfast Bowl
Lunch: Caramelized Onion Lentil and Rice Bowl
Snack: Sweet Potato Chips
Dinner: Cherry Barbecue Chicken Cutlets

Day 7:
Breakfast: Vegan Tofu Scramble
Lunch: Curried Zucchini and Apple Soup
Snack: Pumpkin Rice Patties
Dinner: Moroccan-Spiced Sea Bass

Chapter 1 Breakfast Recipes

26	Blackberry Quinoa Bowl
26	Garlicky Swiss Chard with Fried Eggs
26	Strawberry Spinach Avocado Smoothie
27	Spinach and Mushroom Omelet
27	Cottage Cheese Breakfast Bowl
27	Oatmeal with Apples and Cinnamon
27	Raspberry Banana Smoothie
28	Scrambled Eggs with Arugula and Radish Salad
28	Eggplant Egg Breakfast Sandwich
29	Vegan Tofu Scramble
29	Zucchini and Bell Pepper Frittata
29	Blueberry Chia Oatmeal
30	Tofu Scramble and Roasted Potatoes
30	Huevos Rancheros
31	Herbed Scrambled Eggs
31	Cucumber and Tomato Salad with Egg Whites
31	Vegetable Scramble
32	Greek Yogurt and Berry Bowl
32	Fried Eggs and Lettuce
32	Blueberry Power Breakfast Smoothie

Blackberry Quinoa Bowl

Prep Time: 5 minutes | **Cook Time:** 20 minutes | **Serves:** 2

1½ cups water
Pinch kosher salt
¾ cup quinoa, rinsed

1 cup halved blackberries
Ground cinnamon, for garnish

1. In a medium saucepan, bring the water and salt to a boil over high heat, reduce the heat to low, and add the quinoa.
2. Cook until you see the grains are tender and the liquid is absorbed, about 15 minutes.
3. Remove the quinoa from the heat. If you prefer your quinoa to be fluffy, then cover with a lid for a few minutes and allow it to rest. Once the quinoa is rested, use a fork to fluff it up, top it with the blackberries and a sprinkle of cinnamon, and serve.
4. If you like your grains creamier, serve immediately topped with blackberries and cinnamon.

Per Serving: Calories: 190; Fat: 2.95g; Sodium: 4mg; Carbs: 36.21g; Fiber: 4.95g; Sugar: 3.62g; Protein: 6.28g

Garlicky Swiss Chard with Fried Eggs

Prep Time: 10 minutes | **Cook Time:** 12-15 minutes | **Serves:** 4

2 tablespoons extra-virgin olive oil
5 garlic cloves, minced
2 pounds Swiss chard, stemmed, 1 cup stems chopped fine, leaves sliced into ½-inch-wide strips
1 small red bell pepper, stemmed, seeded, and cut into ¼-inch pieces
Pinch salt
⅛ teaspoon red pepper flakes
4 large eggs
Lemon wedges

1. Heat 1 tablespoon oil and garlic in a 12-inch nonstick skillet over medium-low heat, stirring occasionally, until the garlic is light golden, 3 to 5 minutes. Increase heat to high, add the chard stems, then the chard leaves, 1 handful at a time, and cook until wilted, about 2 minutes. Stir in the bell pepper, salt, and pepper flakes and cook, stirring often, until the chard is tender and peppers are softened, about 3 minutes. Transfer to a colander set in a bowl and let drain while preparing the eggs; discard the liquid. Wipe skillet clean with paper towels.
2. Crack 2 eggs into a small bowl. Repeat with the remaining 2 eggs in the second bowl. Heat the remaining 1 tablespoon oil in the now-empty skillet over medium-high heat until shimmering; quickly swirl to coat the skillet. Working quickly, pour one bowl of eggs in one side of skillet and second bowl of eggs in other side. Cover and cook for 1 minute.
3. Remove the skillet from heat and allow to sit, covered, 15 to 45 seconds for runny yolks (white around edge of yolk will be barely opaque), 45 to 60 seconds for soft but set yolks, and about 2 minutes for medium-set yolks.
4. Divide the chard mixture between individual plates and top with the eggs. Serve immediately with the lemon wedges.

Per Serving: Calories 188; Fat 12.07g; Sodium 701mg; Carbs 12.05g; Fiber 4.1g; Sugar 3.8g; Protein 10.83g

Strawberry Spinach Avocado Smoothie

Prep Time: 5 minutes | **Cook Time:** 0 minutes | **Serves:** 2

2 cups unsweetened non-dairy milk
2 cups baby spinach
1 cup frozen strawberries
½ avocado, peeled and pitted
2 scoops unsweetened vegan protein powder
2 teaspoons pure vanilla extract

1. Place the milk, spinach, strawberries, avocado, protein powder, and vanilla in a blender and blend until smooth. Serve.

Per Serving: Calories: 259; Fat: 11.36g; Sodium: 216mg; Carbs: 21.58g; Fiber: 6.14g; Sugar: 7.82g; Protein: 22.47g

Spinach and Mushroom Omelet

Prep Time: 10 minutes | Cook Time: 10 minutes | Serves: 2

2 large egg whites	Salt and pepper, to taste
1 cup fresh spinach, chopped	Cooking spray
½ cup sliced mushrooms	

1. Heat a nonstick skillet over medium heat and coat with cooking spray.
2. Sauté the mushrooms until softened, about 3 minutes. Add spinach and cook until wilted.
3. Pour in egg whites and let cook undisturbed until set, about 2 minutes.
4. Fold the omelet, season with the salt and pepper, and serve.

Per Serving: Calories: 32; Fat: 0.31g; Sodium: 79mg; Carbs: 2.08g; Fiber: 0.77g; Sugar: 0.54g; Protein: 5.29g

Cottage Cheese Breakfast Bowl

Prep Time: 10 minutes | Cook Time: 0 minutes | Serves: 2

1 cup 2% reduced-fat cottage cheese	2 tablespoons pomegranate seeds or unsweetened dried cranberries
¼ teaspoon orange zest	2 tablespoons roasted unsalted hulled pumpkin seeds (pepitas)
Dash pepper	
1 kiwifruit, peeled and sliced	
¼ cup fresh blueberries	2 tablespoons chopped walnuts

1. In small bowl, mix the cottage cheese, orange zest and pepper. Divide between 2 serving bowls.
2. Divide the remaining ingredients between bowls.

Per Serving: Calories: 238; Fat: 13.67g; Sodium: 365mg; Carbs: 16.79g; Fiber: 3.09g; Sugar: 10.29g; Protein: 15.09g

Oatmeal with Apples and Cinnamon

Prep Time: 2 minutes | Cook Time: 0 minutes | Serves: 2

½ cup rolled oats (cooked in water)	1 teaspoon ground cinnamon
½ cup diced apple	1 tablespoon unsweetened applesauce

1. Cook the oats according to package instructions using water.
2. Stir in the applesauce and cinnamon.
3. Top with the diced apple and enjoy warm.

Per Serving: Calories: 85; Fat: 0.78g; Sodium: 1.50mg; Carbs: 18.74g; Fiber: 2.4g; Sugar: 5.48g; Protein: 2.21g

Raspberry Banana Smoothie

Prep Time: 10 minutes | Cook Time: 0 minutes | Serves: 4

1 cup refrigerated raspberry lemonade	1½ cups fresh raspberries
2 ripe bananas, thickly sliced	2 containers (6 oz each) raspberry fat-free yogurt

1. In blender or food processor, place all ingredients.
2. Cover; blend on high speed about 1 minute or until smooth and creamy. Pour into glasses. Serve immediately.

Per Serving: Calories: 124; Fat: 0.42g; Sodium: 43mg; Carbs: 27.75g; Fiber: 3.46g; Sugar: 21.88g; Protein: 3.58g

Scrambled Eggs with Arugula and Radish Salad

Prep Time: 17 minutes | **Cook Time:** 5 minutes | **Serves:** 4

8 large eggs	2 tablespoons minced red onion
3 tablespoons milk	1 bunch radishes, thinly sliced
Kosher salt	1 lemon, cut into wedges
6 cups arugula	2 tablespoons unsalted butter
1 tablespoon extra-virgin olive oil	

1. In a medium bowl, whisk the eggs, milk, and a pinch of salt until blended. Set aside for 15 minutes.
2. Meanwhile, in a large bowl, toss the arugula with the extra-virgin olive oil, red onion, radishes, and a pinch of salt. Evenly divide the salad among four plates and garnish each with a lemon wedge.
3. Melt the butter in a medium nonstick skillet over medium-high heat. Add the eggs to the skillet and cook by scraping the bottom very slowly, then folding. Repeat until the eggs have formed solid, moist curds. Portion the scrambled eggs evenly among the plates and serve immediately.

Per Serving: Calories: 172; Fat: 12.83g; Sodium: 152mg; Carbs: 4.55g; Fiber: 1.15g; Sugar: 1.89g; Protein: 10.58g

Eggplant Egg Breakfast Sandwich

Prep Time: 5 minutes | **Cook Time:** 20 minutes | **Serves:** 2-4

2 tablespoons extra-virgin olive oil, divided	4 large eggs
1 eggplant, cut into 8 (½-inch-thick) rounds	1 garlic clove, minced
¼ teaspoon kosher salt	4 cups fresh baby spinach
¼ teaspoon freshly ground black pepper	Hot sauce or Harissa (optional)

1. Heat 1 tablespoon of extra-virgin olive oil in a large skillet over medium heat. Add the eggplant in a single layer and cook until tender and browned on both sides, 4 to 5 minutes per side. Transfer the eggplant from the skillet to a plate and season with the salt and pepper. Wipe out the skillet and set aside.
2. Meanwhile, place a large saucepan filled three-quarters full with water over medium-high heat and bring it to a simmer. Carefully break the eggs into small, individual bowls and pour slowly into a fine-mesh strainer over another bowl. Allow the excess white to drain, then lower the strainer into the water. Tilt the egg out into the water. Repeat with the remaining eggs. Swirl the water occasionally as the eggs cook and whites set, about 4 minutes. Remove the eggs with a slotted spoon, transfer them to a paper towel, and drain.
3. Heat the remaining 1 tablespoon of extra-virgin olive oil over medium heat in the large skillet and add the garlic and spinach. Cook until the spinach is wilted, about 1 minute.
4. Place one eggplant round on each of four plates and evenly divide the spinach among the rounds. Top the spinach with a poached egg on each sandwich and place the remaining eggplant round on the egg. Serve with the hot sauce or harissa (if using).

Per Serving: Calories: 133; Fat: 9.75g; Sodium: 145mg; Carbs: 5.85g; Fiber: 2.3g; Sugar: 1.85g; Protein: 7.1g

Vegan Tofu Scramble

Prep Time: 5 minutes | **Cook Time:** 10 minutes | **Serves:** 2

1 (14-ounce) block extra-firm tofu, drained	1 teaspoon minced garlic
2 teaspoons olive oil	2 tablespoons nutritional yeast
½ onion, chopped	¼ teaspoon ground turmeric (optional)
½ red bell pepper, seeded and chopped	Freshly ground black pepper

1. Crumble the drained tofu into a small bowl.
2. In a large skillet, heat the oil over medium-high heat and sauté the bell pepper, onion, and garlic for about 3 minutes, until softened.
3. Add the tofu and sauté for about 4 minutes, until heated through. Stir in the nutritional yeast and turmeric (if using) and toss until the tofu is well coated.
4. Season with the pepper and serve.

Per Serving: Calories: 157; Fat: 7.73g; Sodium: 20mg; Carbs: 8.96g; Fiber: 2.66g; Sugar: 3.05g; Protein: 15.05g

Zucchini and Bell Pepper Frittata

Prep Time: 10 minutes | **Cook Time:** 15-20 minutes | **Serves:** 2

2 large egg whites	1 teaspoon dried oregano
½ cup shredded zucchini	Salt and pepper, to taste
½ cup diced bell peppers	Cooking spray

1. Preheat the oven to 375°F and spray a small oven-safe dish with cooking spray.
2. Mix the egg whites, zucchini, bell peppers, oregano, salt, and pepper in a bowl.
3. Pour the mixture into the dish and bake for 15–20 minutes or until set.
4. Serve warm or at room temperature.

Per Serving: Calories: 27; Fat: 0.28g; Sodium: 86mg; Carbs: 2.25g; Fiber: 0.77g; Sugar: 1.38g; Protein: 4.87g

Blueberry Chia Oatmeal

Prep Time: 2 minutes | **Cook Time:** 8 minutes | **Serves:** 1

8 ounces vanilla soy milk	¼ cup blueberries
½ cup oats	1 tablespoon sliced and toasted almonds
1 tablespoon chia seeds	

1. In a medium saucepan over medium-high heat, stir together the soy milk and oats.
2. Bring to a boil, reduce the heat to low, and simmer, stirring frequently, until cooked and tender, 5 to 8 minutes.
3. Remove the oatmeal from the heat and serve topped with the chia seeds, blueberries, and almonds.
4. Store any leftovers in an airtight container in the refrigerator for up to 5 days.

Per Serving: Calories: 268; Fat: 8.25g; Sodium: 115mg; Carbs: 42.35g; Fiber: 6.55g; Sugar: 8.5g; Protein: 8.85g

Tofu Scramble and Roasted Potatoes

Prep Time: 5 minutes | **Cook Time:** 25 minutes | **Serves:** 4

1½ pounds small potatoes, cut into bite-size pieces	2 teaspoons turmeric
4 tablespoons plant-based oil (safflower, olive, or grapeseed), divided	¼ teaspoon paprika
	1 yellow onion, finely chopped
Kosher salt	1 bell pepper, finely chopped
Freshly ground black pepper	3 cups kale, torn into bite-size pieces
1 ounce water	3 ounces firm tofu, drained and crumbled
2 teaspoons ground cumin	1 avocado, diced, for garnish

1. Preheat the oven to 425°F. Line a baking sheet with parchment paper.
2. Combine the potatoes with 2 tablespoons of oil and a pinch each of salt and pepper on the baking sheet, then toss them to coat. Roast for 20 to 25 minutes or until tender and golden brown.
3. Meanwhile, stir together the water, cumin, turmeric, and paprika until well mixed to make the sauce. Set aside.
4. Heat the remaining 2 tablespoons of oil in a large skillet over medium heat. Add the onion and bell pepper and sauté for 3 to 5 minutes. Season with a pinch of salt and pepper.
5. Add the kale to the skillet, cover, and allow the steam to cook the kale for about 2 minutes.
6. Remove the lid and, using a spatula, push the vegetables to one side of the skillet and place the tofu and sauce on the empty side. Stir until the tofu is heated through, 3 to 5 minutes. Stir the tofu and vegetables.
7. Serve the tofu scramble with the roasted potatoes on the side and garnished with avocado.

Per Serving: Calories: 264; Fat: 16.24g; Sodium: 52mg; Carbs: 26.42g; Fiber: 5.62g; Sugar: 2.91g; Protein: 5.38g

Huevos Rancheros

Prep Time: 10 minutes | **Cook Time:** 15 minutes | **Serves:** 4

1 small onion	1 lime
1 red bell pepper	1 bunch cilantro
2 medium tomatoes or 1 small can (14 fl oz) diced tomatoes	2 tablespoons olive oil
2 cloves garlic	1 tablespoon chipotle peppers in adobo
1 jalapeño pepper	4 eggs
1 can (14 fl oz) black beans	Salt and pepper
1 avocado	Hot sauce (optional, for serving)

1. Chop the onion. Dice the red pepper and tomatoes. Finely chop the garlic and jalapeño. Drain and rinse the black beans. Slice the avocado. Cut the lime into quarters. Chop the cilantro leaves and stems.
2. Heat a large skillet over medium-high. Add the olive oil. Fry the onion and bell pepper for 5 minutes or until softened and aromatic. Stir in the tomatoes, garlic, jalapeño, and chilies in adobo. Add ½ cup/125 mL water or juice from canned tomatoes. Season with the salt and pepper. Simmer for 5 minutes. Stir in the black beans.
3. Make four indentations in salsa. Slide the eggs into indentations, cover, and cook for 5 minutes.
4. To serve, spoon the eggs and salsa into wide, shallow bowls. Garnish with the avocado slices and chopped cilantro. Serve with the hot sauce, if using, and lime wedges.

Per Serving: Calories: 316; Fat: 20.05g; Sodium: 420mg; Carbs: 25.32g; Fiber: 10.04g; Sugar: 4.18g; Protein: 10.75g

Herbed Scrambled Eggs

Prep Time: 5 minutes | **Cook Time:** 3 minutes | **Serves:** 2

4 large eggs	Pinch pepper
2 teaspoons 1 percent low-fat milk	1 teaspoon extra-virgin oil
Pinch salt	2 tablespoons minced fresh chives, basil, and tarragon

1. Beat the eggs, milk, salt, and pepper with a fork in a bowl until the eggs are thoroughly combined and color is pure yellow; do not overbeat.
2. Heat the oil in a 10-inch nonstick skillet over medium-high heat until shimmering, swirling to coat the pan. Add the egg mixture and, using a rubber spatula, constantly and firmly scrape along bottom and sides of skillet until the eggs begin to clump and the spatula just leaves trail on bottom of the pan, 45 to 75 seconds. Reduce the heat to low and gently but constantly fold the eggs until clumped and just slightly wet, 30 to 60 seconds. Quickly fold in the herbs, then immediately transfer the eggs to individual warmed plates. Serve immediately.

Per Serving: Calories: 122; Fat: 9.42g; Sodium: 106mg; Carbs: 1g; Fiber: 0.04g; Sugar: 0.53g; Protein: 8.93g

Cucumber and Tomato Salad with Egg Whites

Prep Time: 10 minutes | **Cook Time:** 0 minutes | **Serves:** 2

1 cup diced cucumber	1 tablespoon lemon juice
½ cup cherry tomatoes, halved	Fresh dill, chopped
3 hard-boiled egg whites, chopped	Salt and pepper, to taste

1. In a bowl, combine the cucumber, tomatoes, and egg whites.
2. Drizzle with the lemon juice, sprinkle with the dill, and season with the salt and pepper.
3. Toss gently and serve chilled.

Per Serving: Calories: 40; Fat: 0.82g; Sodium: 95.50mg; Carbs: 3.48g; Fiber: 0.78g; Sugar: 1.61g; Protein: 5.95g

Vegetable Scramble

Prep Time: 10 minutes | **Cook Time:** 5 minutes | **Serves:** 2

2 cups baby spinach	3 large egg whites
½ cup diced tomatoes	Salt and pepper, to taste
½ cup chopped bell peppers	Fresh parsley, for garnish
½ cup chopped mushrooms	

1. Heat a nonstick skillet over medium heat. Add the bell peppers and mushrooms, cooking until softened, about 3 minutes.
2. Add the spinach and tomatoes, cooking until wilted.
3. Pour in the egg whites and stir gently until cooked through.
4. Season with the salt and pepper, then garnish with the parsley. Serve warm.

Per Serving: Calories: 43; Fat: 0.56g; Sodium: 140mg; Carbs: 4.92g; Fiber: 1.8g; Sugar: 2.75g; Protein: 5.76g

Greek Yogurt and Berry Bowl

Prep Time: 5 minutes | **Cook Time:** 0 minutes | **Serves:** 1

1 cup nonfat plain Greek yogurt	raspberries)
½ cup mixed fresh berries (strawberries, blueberries,	1 teaspoon cinnamon

1. In a bowl, mix the Greek yogurt with cinnamon.
2. Top with the fresh berries and serve immediately.

Per Serving: Calories: 120; Fat: 0.38g; Sodium: 70mg; Carbs: 13.65g; Fiber: 2.98g; Sugar: 8.71g; Protein: 13.45g

Fried Eggs and Lettuce

Prep Time: 5 minutes | **Cook Time:** 2 minutes | **Serves:** 4

4 large handfuls tender lettuce (Boston, mâche, or arugula)	4 pinches of chili flakes
4 tablespoons olive oil, divided	Salt and pepper
4 eggs	

1. Wash and dry the lettuce thoroughly. Heat a heavy skillet with a lid over medium-high heat. When the pan is hot, add 2 table-spoons of olive oil and swirl it around to warm.
2. Crack the eggs into pan, season with the salt and pepper and chili flakes. Cook until the whites have set and edges are browning. Cover and cook the eggs for another 2 minutes to finish the whites.
3. While the eggs are cooking, distribute handfuls of lettuce among four individual plates.
4. To serve, top the lettuce with an egg, spoon the olive oil over each serving, and season with another round of salt and pepper.

Per Serving: Calories 205; Fat 18.13g; Sodium 232mg; Carbs 7.82g; Fiber 4.32g; Sugar 2g; Protein 1.74g

Blueberry Power Breakfast Smoothie

Prep Time: 5 minutes | **Cook Time:** 0 minutes | **Serves:** 1

1 cup unsweetened almond milk, plus more as needed	1 tablespoon extra-virgin olive oil or avocado oil
¼ cup frozen blueberries	1 to 2 teaspoons stevia or monk fruit extract (optional)
2 tablespoons unsweetened almond butter	½ teaspoon vanilla extract
1 tablespoon ground flaxseed or chia seeds	¼ teaspoon ground cinnamon

1. In a blender or a large wide-mouth jar, if using an immersion blender, combine the almond milk, blueberries, almond butter, flaxseed, olive oil, stevia (if using), vanilla, and cinnamon and blend until smooth and creamy, adding more almond milk to achieve your desired consistency.

Per Serving: Calories: 315; Fat: 27.63g; Sodium: 126mg; Carbs: 12.47g; Fiber: 5.22g; Sugar: 4.56g; Protein: 5.47g

Chapter 2 Vegetable and Side Recipes

34	Lemon and Thyme Roasted Vegetables
34	Authentic Moussaka
35	Garlic Roasted Brussels Sprouts with Orange
35	Italian Roasted Vegetables
35	Roasted Grape Tomatoes and Asparagus
36	Greek Roasted Vegetables
36	Oven Roasted Cauliflower with Lemon Tahini Sauce
37	Spiced Roasted Mini Potatoes
37	Garlicky Sautéed Greens
37	Air Fryer Roasted Radishes
38	Garlic Herb Roasted Grape Tomatoes
38	Lemony Green Beans with Red Onions
38	Rosemary Roasted Red Potatoes
39	Slow Cooker Ratatouille
39	Air-Fried Garlic Dill Beets
39	Garlic Roasted Zucchini with Pepper

Lemon and Thyme Roasted Vegetables

Prep Time: 20 minutes | **Cook Time:** 50 minutes | **Serves:** 2

1 head garlic, cloves split apart, unpeeled	½ pint cherry or grape tomatoes
2 tablespoons olive oil, divided	½ fresh lemon, sliced
2 medium carrots	Salt
¼ pound asparagus	Freshly ground black pepper
6 Brussels sprouts	3 sprigs fresh thyme or ½ teaspoon dried thyme
2 cups cauliflower florets	Freshly squeezed lemon juice

1. Preheat the oven to 375°F and set the rack to the middle position. Line a sheet pan with parchment paper or foil.
2. Place the garlic cloves in a small piece of foil and wrap lightly to enclose them, but don't seal the package. Drizzle with 1 teaspoon of olive oil. Place the foil packet on the sheet pan and roast for 30 minutes while you prepare the remaining vegetables.
3. While the garlic is roasting, clean, peel, and trim the vegetables: Cut the carrots into strips, ½-inch wide and 3 to 4 inches long; snap tough ends off the asparagus; trim tough ends off the Brussels sprouts and cut in half if they are large; trim the cauliflower into 2-inch florets; keep the tomatoes whole. The vegetables should be cut into pieces of similar size for even roasting.
4. Place all vegetables and the lemon slices into a large mixing bowl. Drizzle with the remaining 5 teaspoons of olive oil and season generously with the salt and pepper.
5. Increase the oven temperature to 400°F.
6. Arrange the vegetables on the sheet pan in a single layer, leaving the packet of garlic cloves on the pan. Roast for 20 minutes, turning occasionally, until tender.
7. When the vegetables are tender, remove from the oven and sprinkle with the thyme leaves. Let the garlic cloves sit until cool enough to handle, and then remove the skins. Leave them whole, or gently mash.
8. Toss the garlic with the vegetables and an additional squeeze of fresh lemon juice.

Per Serving: Calories 241; Fat 14.43g; Sodium 385mg; Carbs 26.72g; Fiber 8.2g; Sugar 9.27g; Protein 7.07g

Authentic Moussaka

Prep Time: 55 minutes | **Cook Time:** 40 minutes | **Serves:** 6

2 large eggplants	10 cloves garlic, sliced
2 teaspoons salt, divided	2 (15-ounce) cans diced tomatoes
Olive oil spray, or olive oil for brushing	1 (16-ounce) can garbanzo beans, rinsed and drained
¼ cup extra-virgin olive oil	1 teaspoon dried oregano
2 large onions, sliced	½ teaspoon freshly ground black pepper

1. Slice the eggplant horizontally into ¼-inch-thick round disks. Sprinkle the eggplant slices with 1 teaspoon of salt and place in a colander for 30 minutes. This will draw out the excess water from the eggplant.
2. Preheat the oven to 450°F. Pat the slices of eggplant dry with a paper towel and spray each side with an olive oil spray or lightly brush each side with olive oil.
3. Arrange the eggplant in a single layer on a baking sheet. Put in the oven and bake for 10 minutes. Then, using a spatula, flip the slices over and bake for another 10 minutes.
4. In a large skillet add the olive oil, onions, garlic, and remaining 1 teaspoon of salt. Cook for 3 to 5 minutes stirring occasionally. Add the tomatoes, garbanzo beans, oregano, and black pepper. Simmer for 10 to 12 minutes, stirring occasionally.
5. Using a deep casserole dish, begin to layer, starting with eggplant, then the sauce. Repeat until all ingredients have been used. Bake in the oven for 20 minutes.
6. Remove from the oven and serve warm.

Per Serving: Calories: 199; Fat: 10.37g; Sodium: 417mg; Carbs: 25.74g; Fiber: 7.09g; Sugar: 8.92g; Protein: 4.92g

Garlic Roasted Brussels Sprouts with Orange

Prep Time: 5 minutes | **Cook Time:** 10 minutes | **Serves:** 4

1 pound Brussels sprouts, quartered
2 garlic cloves, minced
2 tablespoons olive oil
½ teaspoon salt
1 orange, cut into rings

1. Preheat the air fryer to 360°F.
2. In a large bowl, toss the quartered Brussels sprouts with the garlic, olive oil, and salt until well coated.
3. Pour the Brussels sprouts into the air fryer, lay the orange slices on top of them, and roast for 10 minutes.
4. Remove from the air fryer and set the orange slices aside. Toss the Brussels sprouts before serving.

Per Serving: Calories 127; Fat 7.17g; Sodium 319mg; Carbs 14.71g; Fiber 5.2g; Sugar 5.73g; Protein 4.18g

Italian Roasted Vegetables

Prep Time: 15 minutes | **Cook Time:** 45 minutes | **Serves:** 6

Nonstick cooking spray
2 eggplants, peeled and sliced ⅛ inch thick
1 zucchini, sliced ¼ inch thick
1 yellow summer squash, sliced ¼ inch thick
2 Roma tomatoes, sliced ⅛ inch thick
¼ cup, plus 2 tablespoons extra-virgin olive oil, divided
1 tablespoon garlic powder
¼ teaspoon dried oregano
¼ teaspoon dried basil
¼ teaspoon salt
Freshly ground black pepper

1. Preheat the oven to 400°F.
2. Spray a 9-by-13-inch baking dish with cooking spray. In the dish, toss the eggplant, zucchini, squash, and tomatoes with 2 tablespoons oil, garlic powder, oregano, basil, salt, and pepper.
3. Standing the vegetables up (like little soldiers), alternate layers of eggplant, zucchini, squash, and Roma tomato.
4. Drizzle the top with the remaining ¼ cup of olive oil.
5. Bake, uncovered, for 40 to 45 minutes, or until vegetables are golden brown.

Per Serving: Calories: 147; Fat: 11.98g; Sodium: 124mg; Carbs: 10.01g; Fiber: 4.12g; Sugar: 5.46g; Protein: 1.68g

Roasted Grape Tomatoes and Asparagus

Prep Time: 5 minutes | **Cook Time:** 12 minutes | **Serves:** 6

2 cups grape tomatoes
1 bunch asparagus, trimmed
2 tablespoons olive oil
3 garlic cloves, minced
½ teaspoon kosher salt

1. Preheat the air fryer to 380°F.
2. In a large bowl, combine all of the ingredients, tossing until the vegetables are well coated with oil.
3. Pour the vegetable mixture into the air fryer basket and spread into a single layer, then roast for 12 minutes.

Per Serving: Calories 89; Fat 4.66g; Sodium 196mg; Carbs 11.95g; Fiber 1.8g; Sugar 8.94g; Protein 1.79g

Greek Roasted Vegetables

Prep Time: 15 minutes | **Cook Time:** 40 minutes | **Serves:** 6

2 russet potatoes, cubed	1 teaspoon dried oregano
½ cup Roma tomatoes, cubed	½ teaspoon salt
1 eggplant, cubed	½ teaspoon black pepper
1 zucchini, cubed	¼ teaspoon red pepper flakes
1 red onion, chopped	⅓ cup olive oil
1 red bell pepper, chopped	1 (8-ounce) can tomato paste
2 garlic cloves, minced	¼ cup vegetable broth
1 teaspoon dried mint	¼ cup water
1 teaspoon dried parsley	

1. Preheat the air fryer to 320°F.
2. In a large bowl, combine the potatoes, tomatoes, eggplant, zucchini, onion, bell pepper, garlic, mint, parsley, oregano, salt, black pepper, and red pepper flakes.
3. In a small bowl, mix together the olive oil, tomato paste, broth, and water.
4. Pour the oil-and-tomato-paste mixture over the vegetables and toss until everything is coated.
5. Pour the coated vegetables into the air fryer basket in an even layer and roast for 20 minutes.
6. After 20 minutes, stir well and spread out again. Roast for another 10 minutes, then repeat the process and cook for another 10 minutes.

Per Serving: Calories: 186; Fat: 10.38g; Sodium: 355.83mg; Carbs: 22.41g; Fiber: 4.22g; Sugar: 8.07g; Protein: 3.13g

Oven Roasted Cauliflower with Lemon Tahini Sauce

Prep Time: 10 minutes | **Cook Time:** 20 minutes | **Serves:** 2

½ large head cauliflower, stemmed and broken into florets (about 3 cups)	2 tablespoons freshly squeezed lemon juice
1 tablespoon olive oil	1 teaspoon harissa paste
2 tablespoons tahini	Pinch salt

1. Preheat the oven to 400°F and set the rack to the lowest position. Line a sheet pan with parchment paper or foil.
2. Toss the cauliflower florets with the olive oil in a large bowl and transfer to the sheet pan. Reserve the bowl to make the tahini sauce.
3. Roast the cauliflower for 15 minutes, turning it once or twice, until it starts to turn golden.
4. In the same bowl, combine the tahini, lemon juice, harissa, and salt.
5. When the cauliflower is tender, remove from the oven and toss with the tahini sauce. Return to the sheet pan and roast for 5 minutes more.

Per Serving: Calories: 136; Fat: 9.21g; Sodium: 132mg; Carbs: 11.31g; Fiber: 4.16g; Sugar: 2.79g; Protein: 3.44g

Spiced Roasted Mini Potatoes

Prep Time: 30 minutes | **Cook Time:** 30 minutes | **Serves:** 2

10 ounces golden mini potatoes, halved	½ teaspoon paprika
4 tablespoons extra-virgin olive oil	¼ teaspoon freshly ground black pepper
2 teaspoons dried, minced garlic	¼ teaspoon red pepper flakes
1 teaspoon onion salt	¼ teaspoon dried dill

1. Preheat the oven to 400°F.
2. Soak the potatoes and put in a bowl of ice water for 30 minutes. Change the water if you return and the water is milky.
3. Rinse and dry the potatoes, then put them on a baking sheet.
4. Drizzle the potatoes with oil and sprinkle with the garlic, onion salt, paprika, pepper, red pepper flakes, and dill. Using tongs or your hands, toss well to coat.
5. Lower the heat to 375°F, add the potatoes to the oven, and bake for 20 minutes.
6. At 20 minutes, check and flip the potatoes. Bake for another 10 minutes, or until the potatoes are fork-tender.

Per Serving: Calories: 263; Fat: 14.47g; Sodium: 592.33mg; Carbs: 30.28g; Fiber: 3.44g; Sugar: 1.82g; Protein: 2.92g

Garlicky Sautéed Greens

Prep Time: 10 minutes | **Cook Time:** 5 minutes | **Serves:** 2

1 tablespoon olive oil	dandelion greens, or a combination)
2 garlic cloves, minced	Pinch salt
3 cups sliced greens (kale, spinach, chard, beet greens,	Pinch red pepper flakes (or more to taste)

1. Heat the olive oil in a sauté pan over medium-high heat. Add the garlic and sauté for 30 seconds, or just until it's fragrant.
2. Add the greens, salt, and pepper flakes and stir to combine. Let the greens wilt, but do not overcook. Remove the pan from the heat and serve.

Per Serving: Calories 77; Fat 7.03g; Sodium 301mg; Carbs 3.23g; Fiber 1g; Sugar 0.6g; Protein 1.25g

Air Fryer Roasted Radishes

Prep Time: 5 minutes | **Cook Time:** 18 minutes | **Serves:** 4

1 pound radishes, ends trimmed if needed	½ teaspoon sea salt
2 tablespoons olive oil	

1. Preheat the air fryer to 360°F.
2. In a large bowl, combine the radishes with olive oil and sea salt.
3. Pour the radishes into the air fryer and roast for 10 minutes. Stir or turn the radishes over and roast for 8 minutes more, then serve.

Per Serving: Calories: 56; Fat: 3.5g; Sodium: 297.50mg; Carbs: 5.65g; Fiber: 2g; Sugar: 2.12g; Protein: 0.72g

Garlic Herb Roasted Grape Tomatoes

Prep Time: 10 minutes | **Cook Time:** 45 minutes | **Serves:** 2

1 pint grape tomatoes	½ teaspoon salt
10 whole garlic cloves, skins removed	1 fresh rosemary sprig
¼ cup olive oil	1 fresh thyme sprig

1. Preheat the oven to 350°F.
2. Toss the tomatoes, garlic cloves, oil, salt, and herb sprigs in a baking dish.
3. Roast the tomatoes until they are soft and begin to caramelize, about 45 minutes.
4. Remove the herbs before serving.

Per Serving: Calories: 236; Fat: 20.14g; Sodium: 297mg; Carbs: 14.32g; Fiber: 2.62g; Sugar: 8.83g; Protein: 2.19g

Lemony Green Beans with Red Onions

Prep Time: 5 minutes | **Cook Time:** 10 minutes | **Serves:** 6

1 pound fresh green beans, trimmed	¼ teaspoon black pepper
½ red onion, sliced	1 tablespoon lemon juice
2 tablespoons olive oil	Lemon wedges, for serving
½ teaspoon salt	

1. Preheat the air fryer to 360°F.
2. In a large bowl, toss the green beans, onion, olive oil, salt, pepper, and lemon juice until combined.
3. Pour the mixture into the air fryer and roast for 5 minutes. Stir well and roast for 5 minutes more.
4. Serve with the lemon wedges.

Per Serving: Calories: 53; Fat: 2.9g; Sodium: 208.33mg; Carbs: 6.57g; Fiber: 2.03g; Sugar: 2.1g; Protein: 1.33g

Rosemary Roasted Red Potatoes

Prep Time: 5 minutes | **Cook Time:** 20 minutes | **Serves:** 6

1 pound red potatoes, quartered	¼ teaspoon black pepper
¼ cup olive oil	1 garlic clove, minced
½ teaspoon kosher salt	4 rosemary sprigs

1. Preheat the air fryer to 360°F.
2. In a large bowl, toss the potatoes with the olive oil, salt, pepper, and garlic until well coated.
3. Pour the potatoes into the air fryer basket and top with the sprigs of rosemary.
4. Roast for 10 minutes, then stir or toss the potatoes and roast for 10 minutes more.
5. Remove the rosemary sprigs and serve the potatoes. Season with additional salt and pepper, if needed.

Per Serving: Calories: 136; Fat: 7.5g; Sodium: 199.58mg; Carbs: 16.85g; Fiber: 2.07g; Sugar: 0.8g; Protein: 1.7g

Slow Cooker Ratatouille

Prep Time: 30 minutes | **Cook Time:** 7-9 hours | **Serves:** 6

2 large yellow onions, sliced	1 teaspoon dried basil
1 large eggplant, unpeeled, sliced	2 teaspoons sea salt
4 small zucchini, sliced	¼ teaspoon black pepper
2 garlic cloves, minced	2 tablespoons chopped fresh flat-leaf parsley
2 green bell peppers, cut into thin strips	¼ cup olive oil
6 large tomatoes, cut in ½-inch wedges	

1. Layer one-half of each of the vegetables in the slow cooker in the following order: onion, eggplant, zucchini, garlic, bell peppers, tomatoes. Repeat with the other one-half of the vegetables.
2. Sprinkle with the basil, salt, pepper, and parsley. Drizzle the olive oil over the top.
3. Cover and cook on low for 7 to 9 hours. Serve hot.

Per Serving: Calories: 126; Fat: 7.69g; Sodium: 828.05mg; Carbs: 14.07g; Fiber: 4.18g; Sugar: 8.91g; Protein: 2.64g

Air-Fried Garlic Dill Beets

Prep Time: 10 minutes | **Cook Time:** 30 minutes | **Serves:** 4

4 beets, cleaned, peeled, and sliced	¼ teaspoon salt
1 garlic clove, minced	¼ teaspoon black pepper
2 tablespoons chopped fresh dill	3 tablespoons olive oil

1. Preheat the air fryer to 380°F.
2. In a large bowl, mix together all of the ingredients so the beets are well coated with the oil.
3. Pour the beet mixture into the air fryer basket, and roast for 15 minutes before stirring, then continue roasting for 15 minutes more.

Per Serving: Calories 136; Fat 10.75g; Sodium 210mg; Carbs 10.02g; Fiber 3.1g; Sugar 5.55g; Protein 1.91g

Garlic Roasted Zucchini with Pepper

Prep Time: 5 minutes | **Cook Time:** 15 minutes | **Serves:** 6

2 medium zucchini, cubed	2 tablespoons olive oil
1 red bell pepper, diced	½ teaspoon salt
2 garlic cloves, sliced	

1. Preheat the air fryer to 380°F.
2. In a large bowl, mix together the zucchini, bell pepper, and garlic with the olive oil and salt.
3. Pour the mixture into the air fryer basket, and roast for 7 minutes. Shake or stir, then roast for 7 to 8 minutes more.

Per Serving: Calories: 42; Fat: 2.33g; Sodium: 200.33mg; Carbs: 4.17g; Fiber: 1g; Sugar: 2.17g; Protein: 0.67g

Chapter 3 Grain and Bean Recipes

41	Moroccan Rice and Chickpea Bake
41	Spiced Red Lentils
42	Greek Baked Butter Beans
42	Homemade Refried Beans
42	Brown Rice with Apricots, Cherries, and Pecans
43	Lemony Quinoa with Broccoli and Potatoes
43	Caramelized Onion Lentil and Rice Bowl
43	Lemony Bulgur with Kale and Tomatoes
44	Mushroom Barley Pilaf
44	Baked Brown Rice with Mushrooms and Edamame
45	Tuscan White Beans with Rosemary and Sage
45	Buckwheat and Root Vegetable Bake
46	Lentils with Spinach and Crispy Garlic
46	Sicilian Escarole and White Beans
47	Herbed Barley Pilaf with Mushrooms and Almonds
47	Slow Cooker Vegan Bean Chili

Moroccan Rice and Chickpea Bake

Prep Time: 10 minutes | **Cook Time:** 45 minutes | **Serves:** 6

Olive oil cooking spray
1 cup long-grain brown rice
2¼ cups chicken stock
1 (15.5-ounce) can chickpeas, drained and rinsed
½ cup diced carrot
½ cup green peas
1 teaspoon ground cumin
½ teaspoon ground turmeric
½ teaspoon ground ginger
½ teaspoon onion powder
½ teaspoon salt
¼ teaspoon ground cinnamon
¼ teaspoon garlic powder
¼ teaspoon black pepper
Fresh parsley, for garnish

1. Preheat the air fryer to 380°F. Lightly coat the inside of a 5-cup capacity casserole dish with olive oil cooking spray. (The shape of the casserole dish will depend upon the size of the air fryer, but it needs to be able to hold at least 5 cups.)
2. In the casserole dish, combine the rice, stock, chickpeas, carrot, peas, cumin, turmeric, ginger, onion powder, salt, cinnamon, garlic powder, and black pepper. Stir well to combine.
3. Cover loosely with aluminum foil.
4. Place the covered casserole dish into the air fryer and bake for 20 minutes. Remove from the air fryer and stir well.
5. Place the casserole back into the air fryer, uncovered, and bake for 25 minutes more.
6. Fluff with a spoon and sprinkle with fresh chopped parsley before serving.

Per Serving: Calories: 202; Fat: 2.9g; Sodium: 392mg; Carbs: 37.04g; Fiber: 4.19g; Sugar: 2.05g; Protein: 6.04g

Spiced Red Lentils

Prep Time: 10 minutes | **Cook Time:** 25-30 minutes | **Serves:** 4

Spice Mixture:
½ teaspoon ground coriander
½ teaspoon ground cumin
¼ teaspoon ground cinnamon
¼ teaspoon ground turmeric
⅛ teaspoon ground cardamom
⅛ teaspoon red pepper flakes

Lentils:
1 tablespoon canola oil
4 garlic cloves, minced
1½ teaspoons grated fresh ginger
1 onion, chopped fine
Salt and pepper
3 cups water
1 cup red lentils, picked over and rinsed
12 ounces plum tomatoes, cored, seeded, and chopped
½ cup minced fresh cilantro
1 tablespoon unsalted butter

For the Spice Mixture:
1. Combine all spices in a small bowl.

For the Lentils:
1. Cook the spice mixture, oil, garlic, and ginger in a large saucepan over medium heat, stirring occasionally, until fragrant, about 1 minute. Stir in the onion and ¼ teaspoon salt and cook until softened, about 5 minutes.
2. Stir in the water and lentils, bring to simmer, and cook until the lentils are tender and resemble thick, coarse puree, 20 to 25 minutes. Off heat, stir in the tomatoes, cilantro, butter, and ⅛ teaspoon salt. Season with the pepper to taste and serve.

Per Serving: Calories: 253; Fat: 6.91g; Sodium: 61mg; Carbs: 34.62g; Fiber: 8.75g; Sugar: 6.92g; Protein: 12.65g

Greek Baked Butter Beans

Prep Time: 5 minutes | **Cook Time:** 30 minutes | **Serves:** 4

Olive oil cooking spray	½ yellow onion, diced
1 (15-ounce) can cooked butter beans, drained and rinsed	½ teaspoon salt
1 cup diced fresh tomatoes	¼ cup olive oil
½ tablespoon tomato paste	¼ cup fresh parsley, chopped
2 garlic cloves, minced	

1. Preheat the air fryer to 380°F. Lightly coat the inside of a 5-cup capacity casserole dish with olive oil cooking spray. (The shape of the casserole dish will depend upon the size of the air fryer, but it needs to be able to hold at least 5 cups.)
2. In a large bowl, combine the butter beans, tomatoes, tomato paste, garlic, onion, salt, and olive oil, mixing until all ingredients are combined.
3. Pour the mixture into the prepared casserole dish and top with the chopped parsley.
4. Bake in the air fryer for 15 minutes. Stir well, then return to the air fryer and bake for 15 minutes more.

Per Serving: Calories: 233; Fat: 14.62g; Sodium: 306mg; Carbs: 20.12g; Fiber: 5.34g; Sugar: 3.92g; Protein: 4.46g

Homemade Refried Beans

Prep Time: 5 minutes | **Cook Time:** 15 minutes | **Serves:** 8

3 (15-ounce) cans no-salt-added red kidney beans, rinsed	Salt
1 cup water	2 garlic cloves, minced
2 tablespoons extra-virgin olive oil	1 teaspoon ground cumin
1 onion, chopped fine	¼ cup minced fresh cilantro
1 large jalapeño chile, stemmed, seeded, and minced	

1. Process the beans and water in a food processor until smooth, about 2 minutes, scraping down sides of bowl as needed.
2. Heat 1 tablespoon oil in a medium saucepan over medium heat until shimmering. Add the onion, jalapeño, and ½ teaspoon salt and cook until softened, about 5 minutes. Stir in the garlic and cumin and cook until fragrant. Stir in the bean mixture.
3. Reduce the heat to low and cook, stirring often, until the beans have thickened and flavors meld, about 10 minutes. Off heat, stir in the cilantro and remaining 1 tablespoon oil. Serve.

Per Serving: Calories: 167; Fat: 3.62g; Sodium: 8mg; Carbs: 26.23g; Fiber: 9.06g; Sugar: 1.38g; Protein: 8.23g

Brown Rice with Apricots, Cherries, and Pecans

Prep Time: 10 minutes | **Cook Time:** 55 minutes | **Serves:** 2

2 tablespoons olive oil	4–5 dried apricots, chopped
2 green onions, sliced	2 tablespoons dried cherries
½ cup brown rice	2 tablespoons pecans, toasted and chopped
1 cup chicken stock	Sea salt and freshly ground pepper, to taste

1. In a medium saucepan, heat the olive oil, and add the green onions.
2. Sauté for 1–2 minutes, and add the rice. Stir to coat in the oil, then add the stock.
3. Bring to a boil, reduce the heat, and cover. Simmer for 50 minutes.
4. Remove the lid, add the apricots, cherries, and pecans, and cover for 10 more minutes.
5. Fluff with a fork to mix the fruit into the rice, season with the sea salt and freshly ground pepper, and serve.

Per Serving: Calories: 267; Fat: 10.82g; Sodium: 317mg; Carbs: 39.12g; Fiber: 2.86g; Sugar: 9.27g; Protein: 4.88g

Lemony Quinoa with Broccoli and Potatoes

Prep Time: 10 minutes | **Cook Time:** 5 minutes | **Serves:** 4

2 tablespoons olive oil	2 cups cooked quinoa
1 cup baby potatoes, cut in half	Zest of 1 lemon
1 cup broccoli florets	Sea salt and freshly ground pepper, to taste

1. Heat the olive oil in a large skillet.
2. Add the potatoes and cook until tender and golden brown. Add the broccoli and cook until soft, about 3 minutes.
3. Remove from heat and add the quinoa and lemon zest. Season and serve.

Per Serving: Calories: 218; Fat: 7g; Sodium: 114mg; Carbs: 31.18g; Fiber: 3.1g; Sugar: 1.3g; Protein: 6.03g

Caramelized Onion Lentil and Rice Bowl

Prep Time: 10 minutes | **Cook Time:** 55 minutes | **Serves:** 4

2 cups green or brown lentils	½ teaspoon freshly ground pepper
1 cup brown rice	½ teaspoon dried thyme
5 cups water or chicken stock	¼ cup olive oil
½ teaspoon sea salt	3 onions, peeled and sliced

1. Place the lentils and rice in a large saucepan with water or chicken stock. Bring to a boil, cover, and simmer for 20–25 minutes, or until almost tender.
2. Add the seasonings and cook for another 20–30 minutes, or until the rice is tender and the water is absorbed.
3. In another saucepan, heat the olive oil over medium heat. Add the onions and cook very slowly, stirring frequently, until the onions become browned and caramelized, about 20 minutes.
4. To serve, ladle the lentils and rice into bowls and top with the caramelized onions.

Per Serving: Calories: 493; Fat: 9.5g; Sodium: 303mg; Carbs: 79.25g; Fiber: 13.8g; Sugar: 5.3g; Protein: 16.2g

Lemony Bulgur with Kale and Tomatoes

Prep Time: 15 minutes | **Cook Time:** 8 minutes | **Serves:** 2

2 tablespoons olive oil	2 cups cooked bulgur wheat
2 cloves garlic, minced	1 pint cherry tomatoes, halved
1 bunch kale, trimmed and cut into bite-sized pieces	Sea salt and freshly ground pepper, to taste
Juice of 1 lemon	

1. Heat the olive oil in a large skillet over medium heat. Add the garlic and sauté for 1 minute.
2. Add the kale leaves and stir to coat. Cook for 5 minutes until leaves are cooked through and thoroughly wilted.
3. Add the lemon juice, then the bulgur and tomatoes. Season with the salt and pepper.

Per Serving: Calories: 399; Fat: 14g; Sodium: 62mg; Carbs: 58.35g; Fiber: 11.2g; Sugar: 6.8g; Protein: 10.75g

Mushroom Barley Pilaf

Prep Time: 5 minutes | **Cook Time:** 37 minutes | **Serves:** 4

Olive oil cooking spray
2 tablespoons olive oil
8 ounces button mushrooms, diced
½ yellow onion, diced
2 garlic cloves, minced
1 cup pearl barley
2 cups vegetable broth
1 tablespoon fresh thyme, chopped
½ teaspoon salt
¼ teaspoon smoked paprika
Fresh parsley, for garnish

1. Preheat the air fryer to 380°F. Lightly coat the inside of a 5-cup capacity casserole dish with olive oil cooking spray. (The shape of the casserole dish will depend upon the size of the air fryer, but it needs to be able to hold at least 5 cups.)
2. In a large skillet, heat the olive oil over medium heat. Add the mushrooms and onion and cook, stirring occasionally, for 5 minutes, or until the mushrooms begin to brown.
3. Add the garlic and cook for another 2 minutes. Transfer the vegetables to a large bowl.
4. Add the barley, broth, thyme, salt, and paprika.
5. Pour the barley-and-vegetable mixture into the prepared casserole dish, and place the dish into the air fryer. Bake for 15 minutes.
6. Stir the barley mixture. Reduce the heat to 360°F, then return the barley to the air fryer and bake for 15 minutes more.
7. Remove from the air fryer and let sit for 5 minutes before fluffing with a fork and topping with the fresh parsley.
Per Serving: Calories: 195; Fat: 8.07g; Sodium: 369mg; Carbs: 29.12g; Fiber: 5.19g; Sugar: 2.54g; Protein: 4.73g

Baked Brown Rice with Mushrooms and Edamame

Prep Time: 10 minutes | **Cook Time:** 55-67 minutes | **Serves:** 6

1 cup long-grain brown rice, rinsed
1 tablespoon canola oil
4 ounces shiitake mushrooms, stemmed and sliced thin
4 scallions, white parts minced, green parts sliced thin on bias
2 teaspoons grated fresh ginger
2 cups low-sodium vegetable broth
½ teaspoon salt
1 cup frozen edamame, thawed
1 tablespoon unseasoned rice vinegar, plus extra for seasoning
1 teaspoon toasted sesame oil

1. Adjust the oven rack to middle position and heat the oven to 375 degrees. Spread the rice in an 8-inch square baking dish.
2. Heat the canola oil in a medium saucepan over medium heat until shimmering. Add the mushrooms, scallion whites, and ginger and cook, stirring occasionally, until softened, 5 to 7 minutes. Stir in the broth and salt. Cover the pot, increase the heat to high, and bring to a boil. Once boiling, stir to combine, then immediately pour the mixture over rice. Cover the dish tightly with aluminum foil and bake until the liquid is absorbed and rice is tender, 50 to 60 minutes.
3. Remove the dish from the oven and uncover. Sprinkle the edamame over rice, cover, and let sit for 5 minutes. Add the scallion greens, vinegar, and sesame oil and fluff gently with a fork to combine. Season with the vinegar to taste. Serve.
Per Serving: Calories: 176; Fat: 5.1g; Sodium: 203mg; Carbs: 27.85g; Fiber: 3.13g; Sugar: 2.15g; Protein: 5.63g

Tuscan White Beans with Rosemary and Sage

Prep Time: 10 minutes | **Cook Time:** 10 minutes | **Serves:** 2

1 tablespoon olive oil	1 teaspoon minced fresh rosemary (from 1 sprig) plus 1 whole fresh rosemary sprig
2 garlic cloves, minced	½ cup low-sodium chicken stock
1 (15-ounce) can white cannellini beans, drained and rinsed	Salt
¼ teaspoon dried sage	

1. Heat the olive oil in a sauté pan over medium-high heat. Add the garlic and sauté for 30 seconds.
2. Add the beans, sage, minced and whole rosemary, and chicken stock and bring the mixture to a boil.
3. Reduce the heat to medium and simmer the beans for 10 minutes, or until most of the liquid is evaporated. If desired, mash some of the beans with a fork to thicken them.
4. Season with the salt. Remove the rosemary sprig before serving

Per Serving: Calories: 207; Fat: 7.07g; Sodium: 265mg; Carbs: 26.38g; Fiber: 7.91g; Sugar: 0.95g; Protein: 9.3g

Buckwheat and Root Vegetable Bake

Prep Time: 15 minutes | **Cook Time:** 30 minutes | **Serves:** 6

Olive oil cooking spray	2 rosemary sprigs
2 large potatoes, cubed	1 cup buckwheat groats
2 carrots, sliced	2 cups vegetable broth
1 small rutabaga, cubed	2 garlic cloves, minced
2 celery stalks, chopped	½ yellow onion, chopped
½ teaspoon smoked paprika	1 teaspoon salt
¼ cup plus 1 tablespoon olive oil, divided	

1. Preheat the air fryer to 380°F. Lightly coat the inside of a 5-cup capacity casserole dish with olive oil cooking spray. (The shape of the casserole dish will depend upon the size of the air fryer, but it needs to be able to hold at least 5 cups.)
2. In a large bowl, toss the potatoes, carrots, rutabaga, and celery with the paprika and ¼ cup olive oil.
3. Pour the vegetable mixture into the prepared casserole dish and top with the rosemary sprigs. Place the casserole dish into the air fryer and bake for 15 minutes.
4. While the vegetables are cooking, rinse and drain the buckwheat groats.
5. In a medium saucepan over medium-high heat, combine the groats, vegetable broth, garlic, onion, and salt with the remaining 1 tablespoon olive oil. Bring the mixture to a boil, then reduce the heat to low, cover, and cook for 10 to 12 minutes.
6. Remove the casserole dish from the air fryer. Remove the rosemary sprigs and discard. Pour the cooked buckwheat into the dish with the vegetables and stir to combine. Cover with aluminum foil and bake for an additional 15 minutes.
7. Stir before serving.

Per Serving: Calories: 256; Fat: 9.23g; Sodium: 482mg; Carbs: 39.58g; Fiber: 5.14g; Sugar: 2.79g; Protein: 5.64g

Lentils with Spinach and Crispy Garlic

Prep Time: 10 minutes | **Cook Time:** 49-76 minutes | **Serves:** 4

2 tablespoons extra-virgin olive oil	1 teaspoon ground cumin
4 garlic cloves, sliced thin	2½ cups water
1 onion, chopped fine	1 cup green or brown lentils, picked over and rinsed
Salt and pepper	8 ounces curly-leaf spinach, stemmed and chopped coarse
1 teaspoon ground coriander	1 tablespoon red wine vinegar

1. Cook the oil and garlic in a large saucepan over medium-low heat, stirring often, until the garlic turns crisp and golden but not brown, about 5 minutes. Using a slotted spoon, transfer the garlic to paper towel–lined plate; set aside for serving.
2. Add the onion and ¼ teaspoon salt to fat left in the saucepan and cook over medium heat until softened and lightly browned, 5 to 7 minutes. Stir in the coriander and cumin and cook until fragrant, about 30 seconds.
3. Stir in the water and lentils and bring to simmer. Reduce the heat to low, cover, and cook, stirring occasionally, until the lentils are mostly tender but still intact, 30 to 50 minutes.
4. Stir in the spinach, 1 handful at a time, and cook, stirring occasionally, until the spinach is wilted and lentils are completely tender, about 8 minutes. Stir in the vinegar and ⅛ teaspoon salt and season with the pepper to taste. Transfer to a serving dish, sprinkle with the toasted garlic, and serve.

Per Serving: Calories: 221; Fat: 7.65g; Sodium: 49mg; Carbs: 30.75g; Fiber: 11.28g; Sugar: 3.55g; Protein: 9.68g

Sicilian Escarole and White Beans

Prep Time: 10 minutes | **Cook Time:** 20-32 minutes | **Serves:** 6

2 tablespoons extra-virgin olive oil	1 head escarole (1 pound), trimmed and sliced 1 inch thick
2 onions, chopped fine	1 (15-ounce) can no-salt-added cannellini beans, rinsed
Salt and pepper	1 cup unsalted chicken broth
4 garlic cloves, minced	1 cup water
⅛ teaspoon red pepper flakes	2 teaspoons lemon juice

1. Heat 1 tablespoon oil in a Dutch oven over medium heat until shimmering. Add the onions and ¼ teaspoon salt and cook until softened and lightly browned, 5 to 7 minutes. Stir in the garlic and pepper flakes and cook until fragrant, about 30 seconds.
2. Stir in the escarole, beans, broth, and water and bring to simmer. Cook, stirring occasionally, until the escarole is wilted, about 5 minutes. Increase the heat to high and cook until the liquid is nearly evaporated, 10 to 15 minutes. Stir in the lemon juice and season with the pepper to taste. Drizzle with the remaining 1 tablespoon oil and serve.

Per Serving: Calories: 122; Fat: 4.62g; Sodium: 55mg; Carbs: 17.64g; Fiber: 4g; Sugar: 2.83g; Protein: 4.54g

Herbed Barley Pilaf with Mushrooms and Almonds

Prep Time: 15 minutes | **Cook Time:** 35 minutes | **Serves:** 2

1 tablespoon olive oil	½ cup uncooked pearled barley
1 garlic clove, minced	1½ cups low-sodium chicken stock
3 scallions, minced	½ teaspoon dried thyme
2 ounces mushrooms, sliced	1 tablespoon fresh minced parsley
¼ cup sliced almonds	Salt

1. Heat the oil in a saucepan over medium-high heat. Add the garlic, scallions, mushrooms, and almonds, and sauté for 3 minutes.
2. Add the barley and cook, stirring, for 1 minute to toast it.
3. Add the chicken stock and thyme and bring the mixture to a boil.
4. Cover and reduce the heat to low. Simmer the barley for 30 minutes, or until the liquid is absorbed and the barley is tender.
5. Sprinkle with fresh parsley and season with salt before serving.

Per Serving: Calories: 285.50; Fat: 11.07g; Sodium: 191.50mg; Carbs: 38.59g; Fiber: 6.39g; Sugar: 3.65g; Protein: 9.34g

Slow Cooker Vegan Bean Chili

Prep Time: 20 minutes | **Cook Time:** 4-6 hours | **Serves:** 4

One 28-ounce can chopped whole tomatoes, with the juice	1 teaspoon garlic powder
1 medium green bell pepper, chopped	1 teaspoon cayenne pepper
One 15-ounce can red beans, drained and rinsed	1 teaspoon paprika
One 15-ounce can black beans, drained and rinsed	½ teaspoon sea salt
1 yellow onion, chopped	½ teaspoon black pepper
1 tablespoon olive oil	1 large hass avocado, pitted, peeled, and chopped, for garnish
1 tablespoon onion powder	

1. Combine the tomatoes, bell pepper, red beans, black beans, and onion in the slow cooker. Sprinkle with the onion powder, garlic powder, cayenne pepper, paprika, ½ teaspoon salt, and ½ teaspoon black pepper.
2. Cover and cook on high for 4 to 6 hours or on low for 8 hours, or until thick.
3. Season with the salt and black pepper if needed. Served hot, garnished with some of the avocado.

Per Serving: Calories: 298; Fat: 10.82g; Sodium: 581mg; Carbs: 44.51g; Fiber: 14.97g; Sugar: 6.98g; Protein: 11.83g

Chapter 4 Snack and Appetizer Recipes

49 **Lemon Garlic Shrimp**
49 **Roasted Spiced Chickpeas**
50 **Marinated Mushrooms and Olives**
50 **Sweet Potato Chips**
50 **Crunchy Turmeric Chickpeas**
51 **Crispy Herbed White Beans**
51 **Deviled Eggs with Yogurt and Dill**
51 **Lemon Garlic Hummus**
52 **Air Fryer Popcorn**
52 **Garlic Roasted Tomatoes and Olives**
52 **Roasted Red Pepper Tapenade**
53 **Pumpkin Rice Patties**
53 **Stuffed Cucumber Cups**
53 **Turkish Spiced Mixed Nuts**
54 **Spiced Roasted Cashews**
54 **Herbed Garlic Popcorn**

Lemon Garlic Shrimp

Prep Time: 5 minutes | **Cook Time:** 6 minutes | **Serves:** 4

1 pound medium shrimp, cleaned and deveined	½ teaspoon salt
¼ cup plus 2 tablespoons olive oil, divided	¼ teaspoon red pepper flakes
Juice of ½ lemon	Lemon wedges, for serving (optional)
3 garlic cloves, minced and divided	Marinara sauce, for dipping (optional)

1. Preheat the air fryer to 380°F.
2. In a large bowl, combine the shrimp with 2 tablespoons of the olive oil, as well as the lemon juice, ⅓ of the minced garlic, salt, and red pepper flakes. Toss to coat the shrimp well.
3. In a small ramekin, combine the remaining ¼ cup of olive oil and the remaining minced garlic.
4. Tear off a 12-by-12-inch sheet of aluminum foil. Pour the shrimp into the center of the foil, then fold the sides up and crimp the edges so that it forms an aluminum foil bowl that is open on top. Place this packet into the air fryer basket.
5. Roast the shrimp for 4 minutes, then open the air fryer and place the ramekin with oil and garlic in the basket beside the shrimp packet. Cook for 2 more minutes.
6. Transfer the shrimp on a serving plate or platter with the ramekin of garlic olive oil on the side for dipping. You may also serve with the lemon wedges and marinara sauce, if desired.

Per Serving: Calories: 286; Fat: 21.25g; Sodium: 400mg; Carbs: 2.15g; Fiber: 0.2g; Sugar: 0.4g; Protein: 20.1g

Roasted Spiced Chickpeas

Prep Time: 15 minutes | **Cook Time:** 35 minutes | **Serves:** 2

For the Seasoning Mix:

¾ teaspoon cumin	¼ teaspoon paprika
½ teaspoon coriander	¼ teaspoon cardamom
½ teaspoon salt	¼ teaspoon cinnamon
¼ teaspoon freshly ground black pepper	¼ teaspoon allspice

For the Chickpeas:

1 (15-ounce) can chickpeas, drained and rinsed	¼ teaspoon salt
1 tablespoon olive oil	

To make the seasoning mix:
1. In a small bowl, combine the cumin, coriander, salt, freshly ground black pepper, paprika, cardamom, cinnamon, and allspice. Stir well to combine and set aside.

To make the chickpeas:
1. Preheat the oven to 400°F and set the rack to the middle position. Line a baking sheet with parchment paper.
2. Pat the rinsed chickpeas with paper towels or roll them in a clean kitchen towel to dry off any water.
3. Place the chickpeas in a bowl and season with the olive oil and salt.
4. Add the chickpeas to the lined baking sheet (reserve the bowl) and roast them for about 25 to 35 minutes, turning them over once or twice while cooking. Most should be light brown. Taste one or two to make sure they are slightly crisp.
5. Place the roasted chickpeas back into the bowl and sprinkle them with the seasoning mix. Toss lightly to combine. Taste, and add additional salt if needed. Serve warm.

Per Serving: Calories: 195; Fat: 6.64g; Sodium: 585mg; Carbs: 25.55g; Fiber: 6.23g; Sugar: 2.1g; Protein: 6.79g

Marinated Mushrooms and Olives

Prep Time: 10 minutes | **Cook Time:** 0 minutes | **Serves:** 8

1 pound white button mushrooms	½ tablespoon crushed fennel seeds
1 pound mixed, high-quality olives	Pinch chili flakes
2 tablespoons fresh thyme leaves	Olive oil, to cover
1 tablespoon white wine vinegar	Sea salt and freshly ground pepper, to taste

1. Clean and rinse mushrooms under cold water and pat dry.
2. Combine all ingredients in a glass jar or other airtight container. Cover with the olive oil and season with the sea salt and freshly ground pepper.
3. Shake to distribute the ingredients. Allow to marinate for at least 1 hour. Serve at room temperature.

Per Serving: Calories: 168; Fat: 15.05g; Sodium: 603mg; Carbs: 6.03g; Fiber: 2.04g; Sugar: 1.38g; Protein: 2.2g

Sweet Potato Chips

Prep Time: 5 minutes | **Cook Time:** 15 minutes | **Serves:** 2

1 large sweet potato, sliced thin	2 tablespoons olive oil
⅛ teaspoon salt	

1. Preheat the air fryer to 380°F.
2. In a small bowl, toss the sweet potatoes, salt, and olive oil together until the potatoes are well coated.
3. Put the sweet potato slices into the air fryer and spread them out in a single layer.
4. Fry for 10 minutes. Stir, then air fry for 3 to 5 minutes more, or until the chips reach the preferred level of crispiness.

Per Serving: Calories: 195; Fat: 14g; Sodium: 74mg; Carbs: 17.68g; Fiber: 2.56g; Sugar: 3.96g; Protein: 1.17g

Crunchy Turmeric Chickpeas

Prep Time: 15 minutes | **Cook Time:** 30 minutes | **Serves:** 4

2 (15-ounce) cans organic chickpeas, drained and rinsed	½ teaspoon dried oregano
3 tablespoons extra-virgin olive oil	½ teaspoon salt
2 teaspoons Turkish or smoked paprika	¼ teaspoon ground ginger
2 teaspoons turmeric	⅛ teaspoon ground white pepper (optional)

1. Preheat the oven to 400°F. Line a baking sheet with parchment paper and set aside.
2. Completely dry the chickpeas. Lay the chickpeas out on a baking sheet, roll them around with paper towels, and allow them to air-dry. I usually let them dry for at least 2½ hours, but can also be left to dry overnight.
3. In a medium bowl, combine the olive oil, paprika, turmeric, oregano, salt, ginger, and white pepper (if using).
4. Add the dry chickpeas to the bowl and toss to combine.
5. Put the chickpeas on the prepared baking sheet and cook for 30 minutes, or until the chickpeas turn golden brown. At 15 minutes, move the chickpeas around on the baking sheet to avoid burning. Check every 10 minutes in case the chickpeas begin to crisp up before the full cooking time has elapsed.
6. Remove from the oven and set them aside to cool.

Per Serving: Calories: 290; Fat: 9.52g; Sodium: 379mg; Carbs: 40.74g; Fiber: 8.31g; Sugar: 6g; Protein: 10.89g

Crispy Herbed White Beans

Prep Time: 2 minutes | **Cook Time:** 19 minutes | **Serves:** 2

1 (15 ounce) can cooked white beans	¼ teaspoon garlic powder
2 tablespoons olive oil	¼ teaspoon salt, divided
1 teaspoon fresh sage, chopped	1 teaspoon chopped fresh basil

1. Preheat the air fryer to 380°F.
2. In a medium bowl, mix together the beans, olive oil, sage, garlic, ⅛ teaspoon salt, and basil.
3. Pour the white beans into the air fryer and spread them out in a single layer.
4. Bake for 10 minutes. Stir and continue cooking for another 5 to 9 minutes, or until they reach your preferred level of crispiness.
5. Toss with the remaining ⅛ teaspoon salt before serving.

Per Serving: Calories: 315; Fat: 12g; Sodium: 295mg; Carbs: 38g; Fiber: 9.15g; Sugar: 0.73g; Protein: 11.2g

Deviled Eggs with Yogurt and Dill

Prep Time: 15 minutes | **Cook Time:** 15 minutes | **Serves:** 4

4 eggs	⅛ teaspoon paprika
¼ cup nonfat plain Greek yogurt	⅛ teaspoon garlic powder
1 teaspoon chopped fresh dill	Chopped fresh parsley, for garnish
⅛ teaspoon salt	

1. Preheat the air fryer to 260°F.
2. Place the eggs in a single layer in the air fryer basket and cook for 15 minutes.
3. Quickly remove the eggs from the air fryer and place them into a cold water bath. Let the eggs cool in the water for 10 minutes before removing and peeling them.
4. After peeling the eggs, cut them in half.
5. Spoon the yolk into a small bowl. Add the yogurt, dill, salt, paprika, and garlic powder and mix until smooth.
6. Spoon or pipe the yolk mixture into the halved egg whites. Serve with a sprinkle of fresh parsley on top.

Per Serving: Calories 76; Fat 4.43g; Sodium 152mg; Carbs 2.03g; Fiber 0.6g; Sugar 0.62g; Protein 7.1g

Lemon Garlic Hummus

Prep Time: 15 minutes | **Cook Time:** 0 minutes | **Serves:** 6

1 (15-ounce) can chickpeas, drained and rinsed	1 lemon, zested, divided
4 to 5 tablespoons tahini (sesame seed paste)	1 tablespoon minced garlic
4 tablespoons extra-virgin olive oil, divided	Pinch salt
2 lemons, juice	

1. In a food processor, combine the chickpeas, tahini, 2 tablespoons of olive oil, lemon juice, half of the lemon zest, and garlic and blend for up to 1 minute. After 30 seconds of blending, stop and scrape the sides down with a spatula, before blending for another 30 seconds. At this point, you've made hummus! Taste and add salt as desired. Feel free to add 1 teaspoon of water at a time to help thin the hummus to a better consistency.
2. Scoop the hummus into a bowl, then drizzle with the remaining 2 tablespoons of olive oil and remaining lemon zest.

Per Serving: Calories: 156; Fat: 11.11g; Sodium: 118mg; Carbs: 10.36g; Fiber: 3.26g; Sugar: 0.8g; Protein: 3.57g

Air Fryer Popcorn

Prep Time: 3 minutes | **Cook Time:** 10 minutes | **Serves:** 2

2 tablespoons olive oil
¼ cup popcorn kernels

1 teaspoon garlic salt

1. Preheat the air fryer to 380°F.
2. Tear a square of aluminum foil the size of the bottom of the air fryer and place into the air fryer.
3. Drizzle olive oil over the top of the foil, and then pour in the popcorn kernels.
4. Roast for 8 to 10 minutes, or until the popcorn stops popping.
5. Transfer the popcorn to a large bowl and sprinkle with the garlic salt before serving.

Per Serving: Calories: 170; Fat: 10.5g; Sodium: 588mg; Carbs: 17.5g; Fiber: 3g; Sugar: 0.2g; Protein: 2.5g

Garlic Roasted Tomatoes and Olives

Prep Time: 5 minutes | **Cook Time:** 20 minutes | **Serves:** 6

2 cups cherry tomatoes
4 garlic cloves, roughly chopped
½ red onion, roughly chopped
1 cup black olives
1 cup green olives

1 tablespoon fresh basil, minced
1 tablespoon fresh oregano, minced
2 tablespoons olive oil
¼ to ½ teaspoon salt

1. Preheat the air fryer to 380°F.
2. In a large bowl, combine all of the ingredients and toss together so that the tomatoes and olives are coated well with the olive oil and herbs.
3. Pour the mixture into the air fryer basket, and roast for 10 minutes. Stir the mixture well, then continue roasting for another 10 minutes.
4. Remove from the air fryer, transfer to a serving bowl, and enjoy.

Per Serving: Calories: 97; Fat: 8.21g; Sodium: 332mg; Carbs: 5.67g; Fiber: 1.4g; Sugar: 2.27g; Protein: 0.83g

Roasted Red Pepper Tapenade

Prep Time: 5 minutes | **Cook Time:** 5 minutes | **Serves:** 4

1 large red bell pepper
2 tablespoons plus 1 teaspoon olive oil, divided
½ cup Kalamata olives, pitted and roughly chopped

1 garlic clove, minced
½ teaspoon dried oregano
1 tablespoon lemon juice

1. Preheat the air fryer to 380°F.
2. Brush the outside of a whole red pepper with 1 teaspoon olive oil and place it inside the air fryer basket. Roast for 5 minutes.
3. Meanwhile, in a medium bowl combine the remaining 2 tablespoons of olive oil with the olives, garlic, oregano, and lemon juice.
4. Remove the red pepper from the air fryer, then gently slice off the stem and remove the seeds. Roughly chop the roasted pepper into small pieces.
5. Add the red pepper to the olive mixture and stir all together until combined.
6. Serve.

Per Serving: Calories: 97; Fat: 9.25g; Sodium: 222mg; Carbs: 3.25g; Fiber: 1.15g; Sugar: 1.35g; Protein: 0.75g

Pumpkin Rice Patties

Prep Time: 10 minutes | **Cook Time:** 10 minutes | **Serves:** 6

- 2 cups cooked brown rice
- 1 cup pumpkin puree
- ½ cup finely chopped walnuts
- 3 tablespoons olive oil, divided
- ½ medium onion, diced
- ½ red bell pepper, diced
- 1 teaspoon ground cumin
- Sea salt and freshly ground pepper, to taste
- 1 teaspoon hot paprika or a pinch of cayenne

1. Combine the rice, pumpkin, and walnuts in a large bowl; set aside.
2. In a medium skillet, heat the olive oil over medium heat, add the onion and bell pepper, and cook until soft, about 5 minutes.
3. Add the cumin to the onions and bell peppers. Add onion mixture to the rice mixture.
4. Mix thoroughly and season with sea salt, freshly ground pepper, and paprika or cayenne.
5. In a large skillet, heat 2 tablespoons of olive oil over medium heat.
6. Form the rice mixture into 1-inch patties and add them to the skillet. Cook until both sides are browned and crispy.
7. Serve with Greek yogurt or tzatziki on the side.

Per Serving: Calories 189; Fat 11.86g; Sodium 102mg; Carbs 18.96g; Fiber 2.1g; Sugar 1.68g; Protein 3.22g

Stuffed Cucumber Cups

Prep Time: 5 minutes | **Cook Time:** 0 minutes | **Serves:** 2

- 1 medium cucumber (about 8 ounces, 8 to 9 inches long)
- ½ cup hummus (any flavor) or white bean dip
- 4 or 5 cherry tomatoes, sliced in half
- 2 tablespoons fresh basil, minced

1. Slice the ends off the cucumber (about ½ inch from each side) and slice the cucumber into 1-inch pieces.
2. With a paring knife or a spoon, scoop most of the seeds from the inside of each cucumber piece to make a cup, being careful to not cut all the way through.
3. Fill each cucumber cup with about 1 tablespoon of hummus or bean dip.
4. Top each with a cherry tomato half and a sprinkle of fresh minced basil.

Per Serving: Calories: 123; Fat: 6.75g; Sodium: 214mg; Carbs: 12.8g; Fiber: 3.05g; Sugar: 3.38g; Protein: 3.68g

Turkish Spiced Mixed Nuts

Prep Time: 10 minutes | **Cook Time:** 5 minutes | **Serves:** 4-6

- 1 tablespoon extra-virgin olive oil
- 1 cup mixed nuts (walnuts, almonds, cashews, peanuts)
- 2 tablespoons paprika
- 1 tablespoon dried mint
- ½ tablespoon ground cinnamon
- ½ tablespoon kosher salt
- ¼ tablespoon garlic powder
- ¼ teaspoon freshly ground black pepper
- ⅛ tablespoon ground cumin

1. In a small to medium saucepan, heat the oil on low heat.
2. Once the oil is warm, add the nuts, paprika, mint, cinnamon, salt, garlic powder, pepper, and cumin and stir continually until the spices are well incorporated with the nuts.

Per Serving: Calories: 179; Fat: 15g; Sodium: 284mg; Carbs: 7g; Fiber: 2g; Sugar: 2g; Protein: 5g

Spiced Roasted Cashews

Prep Time: 5 minutes | **Cook Time:** 10 minutes | **Serves:** 4

2 cups raw cashews	¼ teaspoon chili powder
2 tablespoons olive oil	⅛ teaspoon garlic powder
¼ teaspoon salt	⅛ teaspoon smoked paprika

1. Preheat the air fryer to 360°F.
2. In a large bowl, toss all of the ingredients together.
3. Pour the cashews into the air fryer basket and roast them for 5 minutes. Shake the basket, then cook for 5 minutes more.
4. Serve immediately.

Per Serving: Calories: 337; Fat: 28.57g; Sodium: 86mg; Carbs: 17.1g; Fiber: 1.99g; Sugar: 5.09g; Protein: 9.26g

Herbed Garlic Popcorn

Prep Time: 5 minutes | **Cook Time:** 2 minutes | **Serves:** 4-6

3 tablespoons extra-virgin olive oil	⅛ teaspoon dried thyme
¼ teaspoon garlic powder	⅛ teaspoon dried oregano
¼ teaspoon freshly ground black pepper	12 cups plain popped popcorn
¼ teaspoon sea salt	

1. In a large sauté pan or skillet, heat the oil over medium heat, until shimmering, and then add the garlic powder, pepper, salt, thyme, and oregano until fragrant.
2. In a large bowl, drizzle the oil over the popcorn, toss, and serve.

Per Serving: Calories: 101; Fat: 4.42g; Sodium: 97mg; Carbs: 13.88g; Fiber: 2.47g; Sugar: 0.07g; Protein: 1.5g

Chapter 5 Poultry Recipes

56	Poached Chicken Breasts with Tomato-Ginger Vinaigrette
56	Roasted Chicken Breasts with Ratatouille
57	Chicken Shawarma with Chickpeas and Sweet Potato
57	Italian Turkey Meatballs and Zoodles
57	Grilled Lemon Herb Chicken Breasts
58	Slow-Cooked Kofta Casserole
58	Cherry Barbecue Chicken Cutlets
59	Orange Chicken with Pecan Wild Rice
59	Lebanese Grilled Chicken
59	Homemade Chicken Shawarma
60	Mediterranean Slow-Cooked Turkey Breast
60	Braised Chicken with Chickpeas and Chermoula
61	Roasted Chicken with Tzatziki Sauce
61	Shredded Chicken Souvlaki
61	Lemon Herbed Chicken
62	Moroccan-Spiced Chicken with Saffron Rice
62	Moroccan Chicken and Vegetable Tagine
63	Lemon Garlic Chicken Thighs
63	Greek Turkey and Rice Skillet
63	Grilled Chicken and Vegetables with Lemon-Walnut Sauce

Poached Chicken Breasts with Tomato-Ginger Vinaigrette

Prep Time: 10 minutes | **Cook Time:** 20-27 minutes | **Serves:** 4

Chicken:
4 (6-ounce) boneless, skinless chicken breasts, trimmed of all visible fat
½ cup low-sodium soy sauce
6 garlic cloves, smashed and peeled

Vinaigrette:
2 tablespoons extra-virgin olive oil
1 small shallot, minced
1 teaspoon grated fresh ginger
Pinch ground cumin
Pinch ground fennel
6 ounces cherry tomatoes, halved
Salt and pepper
1 tablespoon chopped fresh cilantro
1½ teaspoons red wine vinegar

For the chicken:
1. Pound the chicken breasts to uniform thickness as needed. Whisk 4 quarts water, garlic, and soy sauce together in a Dutch oven. Arrange the breasts, skinned side up, in a steamer basket, making sure not to overlap them. Submerge the steamer basket in water.
2. Heat a pot over medium heat, stirring the liquid occasionally to even out hot spots, until the water registers 175 degrees, 15 to 20 minutes. Turn off the heat, cover the pot, remove from the burner, and let sit until the chicken registers 160 degrees, 17 to 22 minutes. Transfer the breasts to a plate, tent with aluminum foil, and let rest while preparing the vinaigrette.

For the vinaigrette:
1. Heat 1 tablespoon oil in a 10-inch nonstick skillet over medium heat until shimmering. Add the shallot, ginger, cumin, and fennel and cook until fragrant, about 15 seconds. Stir in the tomatoes and ⅛ teaspoon salt and cook, stirring frequently, until the tomatoes have softened, 3 to 5 minutes. Off heat, stir in the cilantro, vinegar, and remaining 1 tablespoon oil. Season with the pepper to taste. Spoon the vinaigrette evenly over each breast before serving.

Per Serving: Calories: 285; Fat: 9.72g; Sodium: 622mg; Carbs: 6.04g; Fiber: 1.24g; Sugar: 2.35g; Protein: 44.77g

Roasted Chicken Breasts with Ratatouille

Prep Time: 10 minutes | **Cook Time:** 30 minutes | **Serves:** 4

1 (14.5-ounce) can no-salt-added diced tomatoes, drained
12 ounces eggplant, cut into ½-inch pieces
1 small zucchini (6 ounces), cut into ½-inch pieces
1 red bell pepper, stemmed, seeded, and cut into ½-inch pieces
2 tablespoons extra-virgin olive oil
4 garlic cloves, halved
1 tablespoon minced fresh thyme or 1½ teaspoons dried
Salt and pepper
2 (12-ounce) bone-in split chicken breasts, trimmed of all visible fat and halved crosswise
1 lemon, quartered
2 tablespoons minced fresh parsley

1. Adjust the oven rack to upper-middle position and heat the oven to 475 degrees. Lightly grease the rimmed baking sheet with canola oil spray. Toss the tomatoes, eggplant, zucchini, bell pepper, oil, garlic, 1 teaspoon thyme, ¼ teaspoon salt, and ¼ teaspoon pepper together in a bowl. Spread the vegetables in an even layer over prepared sheet and roast until beginning to wilt, about 15 minutes.
2. Combine the remaining 2 teaspoons thyme, ¼ teaspoon salt, and ⅛ teaspoon pepper in a bowl. Pound the chicken breast pieces to uniform thickness as needed. Pat dry with paper towels and sprinkle with the thyme mixture.
3. Using a spatula, stir the vegetables, then clear one-quarter of sheet and redistribute vegetables into an even layer. Place the chicken pieces skin side up and lemon wedges cut side down on now-empty portion of sheet. Roast until the vegetables are browned and tender and chicken registers 160 degrees, about 15 minutes, rotating the sheet hallway through roasting. Discard the chicken skin. Toss the vegetables with parsley and any accumulated chicken juices. Serve with the lemon wedges.

Per Serving: Calories: 276; Fat: 11.18g; Sodium: 84mg; Carbs: 10.64g; Fiber: 3.18g; Sugar: 6.32g; Protein: 33.48g

Chicken Shawarma with Chickpeas and Sweet Potato

Prep Time: 10 minutes | **Cook Time:** 20 minutes | **Serves:** 4

1 (15-ounce) can low-sodium chickpeas, drained and rinsed	4 teaspoons store-bought shawarma spice, divided
1 sweet potato, peeled and cut into ½-inch chunks	1 pound boneless, skinless chicken breast, cut into 1-inch chunks
1 tablespoon olive oil	

1. Preheat the oven to 400°F. Line a baking sheet with parchment paper.
2. In a medium bowl, toss the chickpeas, sweet potato, oil, and 1 teaspoon shawarma spice until well combined. Spread the mixture on half of the baking sheet.
3. Add the chicken breast to the bowl and toss with the remaining 3 teaspoons of shawarma spice. Spread the chicken chunks on the other half of the baking sheet.
4. Bake for about 20 minutes, tossing halfway through, until the chicken is cooked through. Serve.

Per Serving: Calories 320; Fat 9.73g; Sodium 531mg; Carbs 22.06g; Fiber 5.9g; Sugar 4.24g; Protein 37.64g

Italian Turkey Meatballs and Zoodles

Prep Time: 10 minutes | **Cook Time:** 20 minutes | **Serves:** 4

1 pound ground turkey	1 teaspoon ground fennel
¼ cup minced onion	½ teaspoon kosher salt
4 tablespoons pitted olives (optional)	Marinara sauce
1 teaspoon dried oregano	8 cups zoodles
1 teaspoon dried thyme	Fresh chopped parsley, for garnish

1. Preheat the oven to 375°F. Line a baking sheet with parchment paper.
2. In a large bowl, combine the turkey, onion, olives, oregano, thyme, fennel, and salt until well mixed. Shape the mixture into 1½-inch meatballs and place them on the prepared baking sheet. Bake for 15 to 20 minutes until the internal temperature of the meatballs reaches 160°F.
3. Meanwhile, heat the marinara sauce in a large saucepan over medium heat. Keep the sauce warm until the meatballs are finished cooking.
4. Transfer the meatballs to the sauce and stir to coat.
5. Place 2 cups of zoodles on each plate and top with the marinara sauce and meatballs. Garnish with parsley and serve.
6. Store any leftovers in an airtight container in the refrigerator for up to 4 days.

Per Serving: Calories: 196; Fat: 8.14g; Sodium: 624mg; Carbs: 13.65g; Fiber: 3.15g; Sugar: 8.04g; Protein: 20.13g

Grilled Lemon Herb Chicken Breasts

Prep Time: 10 minutes | **Cook Time:** 15 minutes | **Serves:** 2

2 tablespoons olive oil	1 teaspoon dried basil
4 tablespoons freshly squeezed lemon juice	½ teaspoon dried thyme
¼ teaspoon salt	¼ teaspoon garlic powder
1 teaspoon paprika	2 (4-ounce) boneless, skinless chicken breasts

1. In a bowl with a lid, combine the olive oil, lemon juice, salt, paprika, basil, thyme, and garlic powder.
2. Add the chicken and marinate for at least 30 minutes, or up to 4 hours.
3. When ready to cook, heat the grill to medium-high (about 350–400°F) and oil the grill grate. Alternately, you can also cook these in a nonstick sauté pan over medium-high heat.
4. Grill the chicken for 6 to 7 minutes, or until it lifts away from the grill easily. Flip over and grill for another 6 to 7 minutes, or until it reaches an internal temperature of 165°F.

Per Serving: Calories: 253; Fat: 13.75g; Sodium: 294mg; Carbs: 2.43g; Fiber: 0.51g; Sugar: 0.31g; Protein: 28.8g

Slow-Cooked Kofta Casserole

Prep Time: 20 minutes | **Cook Time:** 6-8 hours | **Serves:** 4

For the Kofta:

2 pounds raw ground turkey
1 small onion, diced
3 garlic cloves, minced
2 tablespoons chopped fresh parsley
1 tablespoon ground coriander
2 teaspoons ground cumin
1 teaspoon sea salt
1 teaspoon freshly ground black pepper
½ teaspoon ground nutmeg
½ teaspoon dried mint
½ teaspoon paprika

For the Casserole:

Nonstick cooking spray
4 large (about 2½ pounds) potatoes, peeled and cut into ¼-inch-thick rounds
4 large (about 3 pounds) tomatoes, cut into ¼-inch-thick rounds
Salt
Freshly ground black pepper
1 (8-ounce) can no-salt-added, no-sugar-added tomato sauce

To make the kofta:
1. In a large bowl, mix together the turkey, onion, garlic, parsley, coriander, cumin, salt, pepper, nutmeg, mint, and paprika until combined.
2. Form the kofta mixture into 13 to 15 equal patties, using about 2 to 3 tablespoons of the meat mixture per patty.

To make the casserole:
1. Coat a slow-cooker insert with cooking spray.
2. Layer the kofta patties, potatoes, and tomatoes in the prepared slow cooker, alternating the ingredients as you go, like a ratatouille. Season with salt and pepper.
3. Spread the tomato sauce over the ingredients.
4. Cover the cooker and cook for 6 to 8 hours on Low heat, or until the potatoes are tender.

Per Serving: Calories: 414; Fat: 12.56g; Sodium: 627mg; Carbs: 47.32g; Fiber: 6.45g; Sugar: 8.21g; Protein: 32.47g

Cherry Barbecue Chicken Cutlets

Prep Time: 10 minutes | **Cook Time:** 5 minutes | **Serves:** 4

1½ pounds boneless, skinless chicken cutlets
Cherry Barbecue Sauce:
10 ounces pitted fresh cherries
1 small onion, quartered
2 tablespoons Dijon mustard
2 tablespoons red wine vinegar
1½ tablespoons extra-virgin olive oil
1 tablespoon ground fennel seeds
3 chipotle peppers in adobo sauce, plus 1 tablespoon sauce
Pinch freshly ground black pepper

To make cherry barbecue sauce:
1. In a blender, combine the cherries, onion, mustard, vinegar, fennel, chipotle peppers, adobo sauce, and black pepper. Puree until combined and adjust the seasonings as desired.
2. Store in an airtight container in the refrigerator for up to 1 week or in the freezer for up to 3 months.

To make chicken cutlets:
1. Marinate the chicken in half the barbecue sauce in the refrigerator for up to 1 day.
2. The following day, heat the extra-virgin olive oil in a large skillet over high heat. Add the cutlets and cook without disturbing them. Make sure they do not touch, about 1 to 2 inches apart. Cook until brown, 2 to 3 minutes. Flip, and cook another 30 seconds.
3. Repeat with the remaining chicken cutlets if they do not all fit in one pan without overcrowding.
4. Allow the chicken to rest for 5 minutes before serving.
5. Meanwhile, heat the remaining sauce in a small saucepan, then serve with the cooked chicken.

Per Serving: Calories: 297; Fat: 8.67g; Sodium: 179mg; Carbs: 16.34g; Fiber: 2.61g; Sugar: 11.72g; Protein: 36.12g

Orange Chicken with Pecan Wild Rice

Prep Time: 15 minutes | **Cook Time:** 10 minutes | **Serves:** 4

4 boneless, skinless chicken breasts	2 cups wild rice, cooked
Sea salt and freshly ground pepper, to taste	2 green onions, sliced
2 tablespoons olive oil	1 cup pecans, toasted and chopped
Juice and zest of 1 orange	

1. Season the chicken breasts with sea salt and freshly ground pepper.
2. Heat a large skillet over medium heat. Add the oil and sear the chicken until browned on 1 side.
3. Flip the chicken and brown other side.
4. Add the orange juice to the skillet and let cook down.
5. In a large bowl, combine the rice, onions, pecans, and orange zest. Season with the salt and pepper to taste.
6. Serve the chicken alongside the rice and a green salad for a complete meal.

Per Serving: Calories: 471.75; Fat: 22.32g; Sodium: 78.54mg; Carbs: 35.38g; Fiber: 3.21g; Sugar: 4.06g; Protein: 32.17g

Lebanese Grilled Chicken

Prep Time: 10 minutes | **Cook Time:** 14 minutes | **Serves:** 4

½ cup olive oil	2 teaspoons sea salt
¼ cup apple cider vinegar	1 teaspoon Arabic 7 spices (baharaat)
Zest and juice of 1 lemon	½ teaspoon cinnamon
4 cloves garlic, minced	1 chicken, cut into 8 pieces, skinless

1. Combine all the ingredients except the chicken in a shallow dish or plastic bag.
2. Place the chicken in the bag or dish and marinate overnight, or at least for several hours.
3. Drain, reserving the marinade. Heat the grill to medium-high.
4. Cook the chicken pieces for 10–14 minutes, brushing them with the marinade every 5 minutes or so.
5. The chicken is done when the crust is golden brown and an instant-read thermometer reads 180 degrees in the thickest parts. Remove skin before eating.

Per Serving: Calories: 441; Fat: 33.47g; Sodium: 1217mg; Carbs: 3.51g; Fiber: 0.29g; Sugar: 0.39g; Protein: 29.68g

Homemade Chicken Shawarma

Prep Time: 10 minutes | **Cook Time:** 15 minutes | **Serves:** 4

1 pound boneless skinless chicken breasts, cubed	1 teaspoon salt
¼ cup nonfat plain Greek yogurt	¼ teaspoon ground turmeric
2 tablespoons olive oil	¼ teaspoon black pepper
1 teaspoon dried oregano	Rice, for serving (optional)
1 teaspoon ground cumin	Greek salad, for serving (optional)
1 teaspoon ground cinnamon	Tzatziki sauce, for serving (optional)

1. Preheat the air fryer to 380°F.
2. In a large bowl, combine all ingredients and mix together until the chicken is coated well.
3. Spread the chicken mixture in an even layer in the air fryer basket, then roast for 10 minutes. Stir the chicken mixture and roast for an additional 5 minutes.
4. Serve with the rice, a Greek salad, and tzatziki sauce.

Per Serving: Calories: 386; Fat: 12.45g; Sodium: 375mg; Carbs: 34.52g; Fiber: 2.27g; Sugar: 2.32g; Protein: 34.68g

Mediterranean Slow-Cooked Turkey Breast

Prep Time: 15 minutes | **Cook Time:** 6-8 hours | **Serves:** 4

3 garlic cloves, minced	¼ teaspoon ground nutmeg
1 teaspoon sea salt	2 tablespoons extra-virgin olive oil
1 teaspoon dried oregano	2 tablespoons freshly squeezed lemon juice
½ teaspoon freshly ground black pepper	1 (4- to 6-pound) boneless or bone-in turkey breast
½ teaspoon dried basil	1 onion, chopped
½ teaspoon dried parsley	½ cup low-sodium chicken broth
½ teaspoon dried rosemary	4 ounces whole Kalamata olives, pitted
½ teaspoon dried thyme	1 cup sun-dried tomatoes (packaged, not packed in oil), chopped
¼ teaspoon dried dill	

1. In a small bowl, stir together the garlic, salt, oregano, pepper, basil, parsley, rosemary, thyme, dill, and nutmeg.
2. Drizzle the olive oil and lemon juice all over the turkey breast and generously season with the garlic-spice mix.
3. In a slow cooker, combine the onion and chicken broth. Place the seasoned turkey breast on top of the onion. Top the turkey with the olives and sun-dried tomatoes.
4. Cover the cooker and cook for 6 to 8 hours on Low heat.
5. Slice or shred the turkey for serving.

Per Serving: Calories: 429; Fat: 17.36g; Sodium: 634mg; Carbs: 13.32g; Fiber: 2.87g; Sugar: 6.54g; Protein: 55.31g

Braised Chicken with Chickpeas and Chermoula

Prep Time: 10 minutes | **Cook Time:** 24-31 minutes | **Serves:** 4

1½ cups fresh cilantro leaves	Salt and pepper
6 tablespoons extra-virgin olive oil	2 (12-ounce) bone-in split chicken breasts, trimmed of all visible fat and halved crosswise
3 tablespoons lemon juice, plus lemon wedges for serving	2 fennel bulbs, 2 tablespoons fronds minced, stalks discarded, bulbs halved, cored, and sliced thin
4 garlic cloves, minced	¾ cup unsalted chicken broth
1 teaspoon ground cumin	2 (15-ounce) cans no-salt-added chickpeas, rinsed
1 teaspoon paprika	
¼ teaspoon cayenne pepper	

1. Process the cilantro, ¼ cup oil, lemon juice, garlic, cumin, paprika, cayenne, and ¼ teaspoon salt in a food processor until finely ground, about 1 minute, scraping down sides of bowl as needed. Transfer the chermoula to a bowl and set aside for serving.
2. Pound the chicken breast pieces to uniform thickness as needed, pat dry with paper towels, and season with ¼ teaspoon salt and ¼ teaspoon pepper.
3. Heat 1 tablespoon oil in a Dutch oven over medium-high heat until just smoking. Cook the breast pieces skin side down in a pot until well browned, 4 to 6 minutes; transfer to a plate.
4. Heat the remaining 1 tablespoon oil in a now-empty pot over medium heat until shimmering. Add the fennel and cook until softened, about 5 minutes. Stir in the broth, scraping up any browned bits. Stir in the chickpeas and bring to simmer. Nestle the chicken pieces into pot along with any accumulated juices. Reduce the heat to medium-low, cover, and cook until chicken registers 160 degrees, 15 to 20 minutes.
5. Transfer the chicken to the plate and discard skin. Stir the fennel fronds and 1 tablespoon chermoula into the chickpea mixture. Top individual portions of chicken and chickpea mixture evenly with the remaining chermoula. Serve with the lemon wedges.

Per Serving: Calories: 441; Fat: 21.15g; Sodium: 103mg; Carbs: 27.42g; Fiber: 8.24g; Sugar: 3.67g; Protein: 35.26g

Roasted Chicken with Tzatziki Sauce

Prep Time: 6 minutes | **Cook Time:** 24 minutes | **Serves:** 4

4 (4-ounce) boneless, skinless chicken breasts	¼ teaspoon paprika
Sea salt	1 tablespoon olive oil
Freshly ground black pepper	½ cup Tzatziki Sauce, store-bought
1 teaspoon chopped fresh thyme, or ½ teaspoon dried thyme	

1. Preheat the oven to 400°F.
2. Lightly season the chicken breasts with salt and pepper, then cover them in the thyme and paprika.
3. In a large ovenproof skillet, heat the oil over medium-high heat. Brown the chicken breasts on both sides for about 4 minutes in total, turning halfway through.
4. Place the skillet in the oven and roast for about 20 minutes, until cooked through.
5. Serve the chicken breasts topped with tzatziki.

Per Serving: Calories: 207; Fat: 8.96g; Sodium: 193mg; Carbs: 2.62g; Fiber: 0.09g; Sugar: 1.12g; Protein: 28.82g

Shredded Chicken Souvlaki

Prep Time: 10 minutes | **Cook Time:** 6-8 hours | **Serves:** 6

3 pounds boneless, skinless chicken thighs	2 tablespoons extra-virgin olive oil
⅓ cup water	2 teaspoons dried oregano
⅓ cup freshly squeezed lemon juice	¼ teaspoon sea salt
¼ cup red wine vinegar	¼ teaspoon freshly ground black pepper
4 garlic cloves, minced	

1. In a slow cooker, combine the chicken, water, lemon juice, vinegar, garlic, olive oil, oregano, salt, and pepper. Stir to mix well.
2. Cover the cooker and cook for 6 to 8 hours on Low heat.
3. Transfer the chicken from the slow cooker to a work surface. Using 2 forks, shred the chicken, return it to the slow cooker, mix it with the sauce, and keep it warm until ready to serve.

Per Serving: Calories: 311; Fat: 17.92g; Sodium: 161mg; Carbs: 2.03g; Fiber: 0.22g; Sugar: 0.16g; Protein: 33.44g

Lemon Herbed Chicken

Prep Time: 5 minutes | **Cook Time:** 16 minutes | **Serves:** 4

½ cup olive oil	¼ cup chopped flat-leaf parsley
2 tablespoon fresh rosemary	Sea salt and freshly ground pepper, to taste
1 teaspoon minced garlic	4 boneless, skinless chicken breasts
Juice and zest of 1 lemon	

1. Mix all ingredients except the chicken together in a plastic bag or bowl.
2. Place the chicken in the container and shake/stir so the marinade thoroughly coats the chicken.
3. Refrigerate up to 24 hours.
4. Heat a grill to medium heat and cook the chicken for 6–8 minutes a side. Turn only once during the cooking process.
5. Serve with a Greek salad and brown rice.

Per Serving: Calories: 424; Fat: 30.87g; Sodium: 148mg; Carbs: 2.2g; Fiber: 0.3g; Sugar: 0.18g; Protein: 32.95g

Moroccan-Spiced Chicken with Saffron Rice

Prep Time: 15 minutes | **Cook Time:** 15 minutes | **Serves:** 2

For the Chicken:
½ teaspoon paprika
½ teaspoon cumin
½ teaspoon cinnamon
¼ teaspoon salt
¼ teaspoon garlic powder
¼ teaspoon ginger powder
¼ teaspoon coriander
⅛ teaspoon cayenne pepper (a pinch—or more if you like it spicy)
10 ounces boneless, skinless chicken thighs (about 4 pieces)

For the Rice:
1 tablespoon olive oil
½ small onion, minced
½ cup basmati rice, brown
2 pinches saffron
¼ teaspoon salt
1 cup low-sodium chicken stock

To make the chicken:
1. Preheat the oven to 350°F and set the rack to the middle position.
2. In a small bowl, combine the paprika, cumin, cinnamon, salt, garlic powder, ginger powder, coriander, and cayenne pepper. Add chicken thighs and toss, rubbing the spice mix into the chicken.
3. Place the chicken in a baking dish and roast for 35 to 40 minutes, or until the chicken reaches an internal temperature of 165°F. Let the chicken rest for 5 minutes before serving.

To make the rice:
1. While the chicken is roasting, heat the oil in a sauté pan over medium-high heat. Add the onion and sauté for 5 minutes.
2. Add the rice, saffron, salt, and chicken stock. Cover the pot with a tight-fitting lid and reduce the heat to low. Let the rice simmer for 15 minutes, or until it is light and fluffy and the liquid has been absorbed.

Per Serving: Calories: 386; Fat: 12.45g; Sodium: 375mg; Carbs: 34.52g; Fiber: 2.27g; Sugar: 2.32g; Protein: 34.68g

Moroccan Chicken and Vegetable Tagine

Prep Time: 10 minutes | **Cook Time:** 1 hour | **Serves:** 6

½ cup extra-virgin olive oil, divided
1½ pounds boneless skinless chicken thighs, cut into 1-inch chunks
1½ teaspoons salt, divided
½ teaspoon freshly ground black pepper
1 small red onion, chopped
1 red bell pepper, cut into 1-inch squares
2 medium tomatoes, chopped or 1½ cups diced canned tomatoes
1 cup water
2 medium zucchini, sliced into ¼-inch-thick half moons
1 cup pitted halved olives (Kalamata or Spanish green work nicely)
¼ cup chopped fresh cilantro or flat-leaf Italian parsley
Riced cauliflower or sautéed spinach, for serving

1. In a Dutch oven or large rimmed skillet, heat ¼ cup olive oil over medium-high heat.
2. Season the chicken with 1 teaspoon salt and pepper and sauté until just browned on all sides, 6 to 8 minutes.
3. Add the onions and peppers and sauté until wilted, another 6 to 8 minutes.
4. Add the chopped tomatoes and water, bring to a boil, and reduce the heat to low. Cover and simmer over low heat until the meat is cooked through and very tender, 30 to 45 minutes.
5. Add the remaining ¼ cup olive oil, zucchini, olives, and cilantro, stirring to combine. Continue to cook over low heat, uncovered, until the zucchini is tender, about 10 minutes.
6. Serve warm over the riced cauliflower or atop a bed of sautéed spinach.

Per Serving: Calories: 326.67; Fat: 22.17g; Sodium: 702mg; Carbs: 7.48g; Fiber: 2.05g; Sugar: 3.04g; Protein: 23.41g

Lemon Garlic Chicken Thighs

Prep Time: 10 minutes | **Cook Time:** 6-8 hours | **Serves:** 6

3 pounds boneless, skinless chicken thighs	1 teaspoon extra-virgin olive oil
½ cup low-sodium chicken broth	1 teaspoon sea salt
¼ cup freshly squeezed lemon juice	½ teaspoon freshly ground black pepper
4 garlic cloves, minced	½ teaspoon dried thyme, parsley, or basil (or other herb of your choice)
1 teaspoon grated lemon zest	

1. In a slow cooker, combine the chicken, chicken broth, lemon juice, garlic, lemon zest, olive oil, salt, pepper, and your preferred herb. Stir to mix well.
2. Cover the cooker and cook for 6 to 8 hours on Low heat.

Per Serving: Calories 290; Fat 10.26g; Sodium 610mg; Carbs 1.81g; Fiber 0.1g; Sugar 0.32g; Protein 45.18g

Greek Turkey and Rice Skillet

Prep Time: 20 minutes | **Cook Time:** 30 minutes | **Serves:** 2

1 tablespoon olive oil	1 teaspoon dried oregano
½ medium onion, minced	½ cup brown rice
2 garlic cloves, minced	1¼ cups low-sodium chicken stock
8 ounces ground turkey breast	Salt
½ cup roasted red peppers, chopped (about 2 jarred peppers)	2 cups lightly packed baby spinach
¼ cup sun-dried tomatoes, minced	

1. Heat the olive oil in a sauté pan over medium heat. Add the onion and sauté for 5 minutes. Add the garlic and cook for another 30 seconds.
2. Add the turkey breast and cook for 7 minutes, breaking the turkey up with a spoon, until no longer pink.
3. Add the roasted red peppers, sun-dried tomatoes, and oregano and stir to combine. Add the rice and chicken stock and bring the mixture to a boil.
4. Cover the pan and reduce the heat to medium-low. Simmer for 30 minutes, or until the rice is cooked and tender. Season with the salt.
5. Add the spinach to the pan and stir until it wilts slightly.

Per Serving: Calories: 353; Fat: 11.5g; Sodium: 273mg; Carbs: 34.1g; Fiber: 3.68g; Sugar: 6.23g; Protein: 30.1g

Grilled Chicken and Vegetables with Lemon–Walnut Sauce

Prep Time: 20 minutes | **Cook Time:** 16 minutes | **Serves:** 4

1 cup chopped walnuts, toasted	Sea salt and freshly ground pepper, to taste
1 small shallot, very finely chopped	2 zucchini, sliced diagonally ¼-inch thick
½ cup olive oil, plus more for brushing	½ pound asparagus
Juice and zest of 1 lemon	1 red onion, sliced ⅓-inch thick
4 boneless, skinless chicken breasts	1 teaspoon Italian seasoning

1. Preheat a grill to medium-high.
2. Put the walnuts, shallots, olive oil, lemon juice, and lemon zest in a food processor and process until smooth and creamy.
3. Season the chicken with sea salt and freshly ground pepper, and grill on an oiled grate until cooked through, about 7–8 minutes a side or until an instant-read thermometer reaches 180 degrees in the thickest part.
4. When the chicken is halfway done, put the vegetables on the grill. Sprinkle the Italian seasoning over the chicken and vegetables to taste.
5. To serve, lay the grilled veggies on a plate, place the chicken breast on the grilled vegetables, and spoon the lemon-walnut sauce over the chicken and vegetables.

Per Serving: Calories: 568; Fat: 44.26g; Sodium: 60mg; Carbs: 14.63g; Fiber: 3.99g; Sugar: 5.73g; Protein: 30.57g

Chapter 6 Beef, Pork, and Lamb Recipes

- 65 Roasted Pork Tenderloin with Chermoula Sauce
- 65 Greek-Style Lamb Chops
- 65 Roasted Herbed Beef Tips
- 66 Grilled Spiced Pork Tenderloin
- 66 Braised Lamb Shanks in Herbed Tomato Sauce
- 66 Beef Osso Buco
- 67 Thyme Grilled Pork Chops
- 67 Braised Beef Brisket with Onions
- 67 Slow Cooker Italian Beef Ragù
- 68 Slow-Cooked Herbed Leg of Lamb
- 68 Balsamic Rosemary Pork Tenderloin
- 68 Herb-Marinated Grilled Flank Steak
- 69 Spinach Stuffed Flank Steak
- 69 Mediterranean Pork Chops with Olives
- 70 Lemon Herb-Crusted Pork Tenderloin
- 70 Roasted Pork Tenderloin with Cherry-Balsamic Sauce
- 71 Kofta with Vegetables in Tomato Sauce
- 71 Slow-Cooked Moroccan Lamb Roast
- 72 Moroccan Lamb Shanks and Potatoes
- 72 Grilled Greek-Inspired Beef Kebabs

Roasted Pork Tenderloin with Chermoula Sauce

Prep Time: 15 minutes | **Cook Time:** 20 minutes | **Serves:** 2

½ cup fresh parsley	1 teaspoon smoked paprika
½ cup fresh cilantro	2 teaspoons cumin
6 small garlic cloves	½ teaspoon salt, divided
3 tablespoons olive oil, divided	Pinch freshly ground black pepper
3 tablespoons freshly squeezed lemon juice	1 (8-ounce) pork tenderloin, trimmed of visible fat

1. Preheat the oven to 425°F and set the rack to the middle position.
2. In the bowl of a food processor, combine the parsley, cilantro, garlic, 2 tablespoons of olive oil, the lemon juice, paprika, cumin, and ¼ teaspoon of salt. Pulse 15 to 20 times, or until the mixture is fairly smooth. Scrape the sides down as needed to incorporate all of the ingredients. Transfer the sauce to a small bowl and set aside.
3. Season the pork tenderloin on all sides with the remaining ¼ teaspoon of salt and a generous pinch of pepper.
4. Heat the remaining 1 tablespoon of olive oil in a sauté pan. Add the pork and sear for 3 minutes, turning often, until it's golden on all sides.
5. Transfer the pork to an oven-safe baking dish and roast for 15 minutes, or until the internal temperature registers 145°F.

Per Serving: Calories: 277; Fat: 16.47g; Sodium: 333mg; Carbs: 4.17g; Fiber: 1.43g; Sugar: 0.78g; Protein: 28.85g

Greek-Style Lamb Chops

Prep Time: 10 minutes | **Cook Time:** 6-8 hours | **Serves:** 6

3 pounds lamb chops, trimmed of visible fat	2 garlic cloves, minced
½ cup low-sodium beef broth	1 teaspoon dried oregano
Juice of 1 lemon	1 teaspoon sea salt
1 tablespoon extra-virgin olive oil	½ teaspoon freshly ground black pepper

1. Put the lamb chops in a slow cooker.
2. In a small bowl, whisk together the beef broth, lemon juice, olive oil, garlic, oregano, salt, and pepper until blended. Pour the sauce over the lamb chops.
3. Cover the cooker and cook for 6 to 8 hours on Low heat.

Per Serving: Calories: 378; Fat: 23.6g; Sodium: 432mg; Carbs: 1.2g; Fiber: 0.25g; Sugar: 0.18g; Protein: 38.23g

Roasted Herbed Beef Tips

Prep Time: 5 minutes | **Cook Time:** 10 minutes | **Serves:** 4

1 pound rib eye steak, cubed	1 teaspoon salt
2 garlic cloves, minced	½ teaspoon black pepper
2 tablespoons olive oil	1 yellow onion, thinly sliced
1 tablespoon fresh oregano	

1. Preheat the air fryer to 380°F.
2. In a medium bowl, combine the steak, garlic, olive oil, oregano, salt, pepper, and onion. Mix until all of the beef and onion are well coated.
3. Put the seasoned steak mixture into the air fryer basket. Roast for 5 minutes. Stir and roast for 5 minutes more.
4. Let rest for 5 minutes before serving with some favorite sides.

Per Serving: Calories: 372; Fat: 23.98g; Sodium: 655mg; Carbs: 4.38g; Fiber: 0.86g; Sugar: 1.43g; Protein: 33.25g

Grilled Spiced Pork Tenderloin

Prep Time: 10 minutes | **Cook Time:** 12 minutes | **Serves:** 6

2 tablespoons olive oil	½ teaspoon ginger
1 teaspoon Spanish paprika	½ teaspoon freshly ground pepper
1 teaspoon red wine vinegar	¼ teaspoon turmeric
1 clove garlic, minced	1 pound pork tenderloin, trimmed of visible fat
½ teaspoon ground cumin	Sea salt and freshly ground pepper, to taste
½ teaspoon ground coriander	

1. Combine all the ingredients except the pork tenderloin.
2. Spread over the meat in a thick paste, cover, and refrigerate for several hours or overnight.
3. Heat a grill to medium heat, and grill the tenderloin for 10–12 minutes, turning halfway through. An instant-read thermometer should read 145 degrees.
4. Transfer the tenderloin to a serving platter, and allow it to rest for 15 minutes before slicing.
5. Season to taste and serve.

Per Serving: Calories: 151; Fat: 6.23g; Sodium: 159mg; Carbs: 1.12g; Fiber: 0.28g; Sugar: 0g; Protein: 21.99g

Braised Lamb Shanks in Herbed Tomato Sauce

Prep Time: 10 minutes | **Cook Time:** 8-10 hours | **Serves:** 4

1 onion, diced	1 cup low-sodium beef broth
1 (28-ounce) no-salt-added, whole peeled tomatoes, with juice	1 teaspoon sea salt
	1 teaspoon dried rosemary
2 large carrots, diced	1 teaspoon dried thyme
3 garlic cloves, minced	4 lamb shanks (about 3 pounds), trimmed

1. In a slow cooker, combine the onion, tomatoes and their juice, carrots, garlic, beef broth, salt, rosemary, and thyme. Stir to mix well.
2. Nestle the lamb shanks into the tomato mixture.
3. Cover the cooker and cook for 8 to 10 hours on Low heat.

Per Serving: Calories: 450; Fat: 20.12g; Sodium: 513mg; Carbs: 16.05g; Fiber: 3.45g; Sugar: 7.63g; Protein: 49.43g

Beef Osso Buco

Prep Time: 10 minutes | **Cook Time:** 8-10 hours | **Serves:** 4

1 (15-ounce) can no-salt-added diced tomatoes	2 garlic cloves, minced
1 cup low-sodium beef broth	1 teaspoon sea salt
2 carrots, diced	2 to 3 pounds bone-in beef shanks, trimmed of visible fat
1 small onion, diced	2 tablespoons Italian seasoning
1 celery stalk, diced	Handful fresh parsley

1. In a slow cooker, combine the tomatoes, beef broth, carrots, onion, celery, garlic, and salt. Stir to mix well.
2. Generously season the beef shanks with the Italian seasoning. Nestle the shanks into the vegetable mixture.
3. Cover the cooker and cook for 8 to 10 hours on Low heat.
4. Garnish with the fresh parsley for serving.

Per Serving: 289; Fat: 9.25g; Sodium: 774mg; Carbs: 13.54g; Fiber: 3.38g; Sugar: 6.41g; Protein: 36.69g

Thyme Grilled Pork Chops

Prep Time: 20 minutes | **Cook Time:** 10 minutes | **Serves:** 4

- ¼ cup extra-virgin olive oil
- 1 teaspoon smoked paprika
- 2 tablespoons fresh thyme leaves
- 1 teaspoon salt
- 4 pork loin chops, ½-inch-thick, trimmed of visible fat

1. In a small bowl, mix together the olive oil, paprika, thyme, and salt.
2. Put the pork chops in a plastic zip-top bag or a bowl and coat them with the spice mix. Let them marinate for 15 minutes.
3. Preheat a grill, grill pan, or lightly oiled skillet to high heat. Cook the pork chops for 4 minutes on each side. Serve with a Greek salad.

Per Serving: Calories: 328; Fat: 23.15g; Sodium: 604mg; Carbs: 1.65g; Fiber: 0.5g; Sugar: 0g; Protein: 27.85g

Braised Beef Brisket with Onions

Prep Time: 10 minutes | **Cook Time:** 6 hours | **Serves:** 6

- 1 large yellow onion, thinly sliced
- 2 garlic cloves, smashed and peeled
- 1 first cut of beef brisket (4 pounds), trimmed of excess fat
- Coarse sea salt
- Black pepper
- 2 cups chicken broth
- 2 tablespoons chopped fresh parsley leaves, for serving

1. Combine the onion and garlic in the slow cooker.
2. Season the brisket with salt and pepper, and place, fat-side up, in the slow cooker.
3. Add the broth to the slow cooker. Cover and cook until the brisket is fork-tender, on high for about 6 hours.
4. Transfer the brisket to a cutting board and thinly slice across the grain.
5. Serve with the onion and some cooking liquid, sprinkled with the parsley.

Per Serving: Calories: 416; Fat: 24.35g; Sodium: 449mg; Carbs: 3.67g; Fiber: 0.6g; Sugar: 1.13g; Protein: 43.97g

Slow Cooker Italian Beef Ragù

Prep Time: 15 minutes | **Cook Time:** 4½ hours | **Serves:** 6

- 1 medium yellow onion, diced small
- 3 cloves garlic, minced
- 6 tablespoons tomato paste
- 3 tablespoons chopped fresh oregano leaves (or 3 teaspoons dried oregano)
- One 4-pound beef chuck roast, halved, trimmed
- Coarse sea salt
- Black pepper
- 2 cups beef stock
- 2 tablespoons red wine vinegar

1. Combine the onion, garlic, tomato paste, and oregano in the slow cooker.
2. Season the roast halves with salt and pepper and place on top of the onion mixture in the slow cooker. Add the beef stock.
3. Cover and cook until meat is tender and can easily be pulled apart with a fork, on high for 4½ hours, or on low for 9 hours. Let cool 10 minutes.
4. Shred the meat while it is still in the slow cooker using two forks. Stir the vinegar into the sauce. Serve hot, over the pasta.

Per Serving: Calories: 412; Fat: 20.23g; Sodium: 472mg; Carbs: 6.12g; Fiber: 1.08g; Sugar: 2.18g; Protein: 49.02g

Slow-Cooked Herbed Leg of Lamb

Prep Time: 10 minutes | **Cook Time:** 8-10 hours | **Serves:** 6

2 cups low-sodium beef broth	3 large garlic cloves, minced
2 rosemary sprigs (optional)	1½ teaspoons dried rosemary
1 (3- to 4-pound) bone-in lamb leg, trimmed of visible fat	1 teaspoon sea salt
1 tablespoon extra-virgin olive oil	½ teaspoon freshly ground black pepper

1. In a slow cooker, combine the beef broth and rosemary sprigs (if using).
2. Rub the lamb all over with olive oil and season with garlic, rosemary, salt, and pepper. Add the lamb to the slow cooker.
3. Cover the cooker and cook for 8 to 10 hours on Low heat, or until the lamb is tender.

Per Serving: Calories: 357; Fat: 19.34g; Sodium: 476mg; Carbs: 1.1g; Fiber: 0.21g; Sugar: 0.14g; Protein: 43.15g

Balsamic Rosemary Pork Tenderloin

Prep Time: 10 minutes | **Cook Time:** 6-8 hours | **Serves:** 6

1 small onion, sliced	2 tablespoons capers, undrained
1 (3-pound) pork tenderloin, trimmed of visible fat	1½ teaspoons olive oil
1 cup balsamic vinegar	1 teaspoon dried rosemary
½ cup low-sodium beef broth	1 teaspoon sea salt
3 garlic cloves, crushed	½ teaspoon freshly ground black pepper

1. Put the onion in a slow cooker and arrange the pork tenderloin on top.
2. In a small bowl, whisk together the vinegar, beef broth, garlic, capers, olive oil, rosemary, salt, and pepper until combined. Pour the sauce over the pork.
3. Cover the cooker and cook for 6 to 8 hours on Low heat.

Per Serving: Calories: 259; Fat: 8.68g; Sodium: 570mg; Carbs: 12.59g; Fiber: 0.89g; Sugar: 10.13g; Protein: 30.6g

Herb-Marinated Grilled Flank Steak

Prep Time: 10 minutes | **Cook Time:** 18 minutes | **Serves:** 6

¼ cup olive oil	1 teaspoon paprika
3 tablespoons red wine vinegar	2 cloves garlic, minced
1 teaspoon dried rosemary	1 teaspoon freshly ground pepper
1 teaspoon dried marjoram	2 pounds flank steak
1 teaspoon dried oregano	

1. Combine the olive oil, vinegar, herbs, and seasonings in a small bowl. Put the flank steak in a shallow dish, and rub the marinade into the meat. Cover and refrigerate for up to 24 hours.
2. Heat a charcoal or gas grill to medium heat (350–375 degrees).
3. Grill the steak for 18–21 minutes, turning once halfway through the cooking time.
4. An internal meat thermometer should read 135–140 degrees when the meat is done.
5. Transfer the meat to a cutting board, and cover with aluminum foil. Let steak rest for at least 10 minutes.
6. Slice against the grain very thinly and serve.

Per Serving: Calories: 297; Fat: 18.17g; Sodium: 45mg; Carbs: 2.1g; Fiber: 0.62g; Sugar: 0.56g; Protein: 30.9g

Spinach Stuffed Flank Steak

Prep Time: 20 minutes | **Cook Time:** 6 hours | **Serves:** 6

2 pounds flank steak	½ cup dried tomatoes, chopped
Sea salt and freshly ground pepper, to taste	½ cup roasted red peppers, diced
1 tablespoon olive oil	½ cup almonds, toasted and chopped
¼ cup onion, diced	½ cup chicken stock
1 clove garlic, minced	Kitchen twine
2 cups baby spinach, chopped	

1. Lay the flank steak out on a cutting board, and generously season with the sea salt and freshly ground pepper
2. In a medium saucepan, heat the olive oil. Add the onion and garlic.
3. Cook for 5 minutes on medium heat, or until the onion is tender and translucent, stirring frequently.
4. Add the spinach, tomatoes, peppers, and chopped almonds, and cook for another 3 minutes, or until the spinach wilts slightly.
5. Allow the tomato and spinach mixture to cool to room temperature. Spread the tomato and spinach mixture evenly over the flank steak.
6. Roll the flank steak up slowly, and tie it securely with kitchen twine on both ends and in the middle.
7. Brown the flank steak in the same pan for 5 minutes, turning it carefully to brown all sides.
8. Place steak in a slow cooker with the chicken stock. Cover and cook on low for 4–6 hours.
9. Cut into rounds, discarding the twine, and serve.

Per Serving: Calories: 313; Fat: 16.52g; Sodium: 134mg; Carbs: 9.34g; Fiber: 3.02g; Sugar: 3.12g; Protein: 31.47g

Mediterranean Pork Chops with Olives

Prep Time: 10 minutes | **Cook Time:** 6-8 hours | **Serves:** 4

1 small onion, sliced	1 teaspoon dried oregano
4 thick-cut, bone-in pork chops, trimmed of visible fat	1 teaspoon dried parsley
1 cup low-sodium chicken broth	½ teaspoon freshly ground black pepper
Juice of 1 lemon	2 cups whole green olives, pitted
2 garlic cloves, minced	1 pint cherry tomatoes
1 teaspoon sea salt	

1. Put the onion in a slow cooker and arrange the pork chops on top.
2. In a small bowl, whisk together the chicken broth, lemon juice, garlic, salt, oregano, parsley, and pepper. Pour the sauce over the pork chops. Top with the olives and tomatoes.
3. Cover the cooker and cook for 6 to 8 hours on Low heat.

Per Serving: Calories: 314; Fat: 18.04g; Sodium: 982mg; Carbs: 10.56g; Fiber: 2.61g; Sugar: 4.28g; Protein: 28.47g

Lemon Herb–Crusted Pork Tenderloin

Prep Time: 10 minutes | **Cook Time:** 20 minutes | **Serves:** 2

1 (8-ounce) pork tenderloin, trimmed of visible fat	¼ teaspoon za'atar seasoning
Zest of 1 lemon	¼ teaspoon salt
½ teaspoon dried thyme	1 tablespoon olive oil
¼ teaspoon garlic powder	

1. Preheat the oven to 425°F and set the rack to the middle position.
2. Trim away any of the silver skin from the pork tenderloin, to prevent it from curling while it cooks.
3. Combine the lemon zest, thyme, garlic powder, za'atar, and salt in a small bowl. Rub it evenly over the pork tenderloin.
4. Heat the olive oil in a sauté pan over medium-high heat. Add the pork and sauté for 3 minutes, turning often, until it's golden on all sides.
5. Place the tenderloin in an oven-safe baking dish and roast for 15 minutes, or until the internal temperature registers 145°F. Remove it from the oven and let it rest for 3 minutes before serving.

Per Serving: Calories: 211; Fat: 10.3g; Sodium: 266mg; Carbs: 1.05g; Fiber: 0.2g; Sugar: 0.09g; Protein: 27.51g

Roasted Pork Tenderloin with Cherry–Balsamic Sauce

Prep Time: 20 minutes | **Cook Time:** 20 minutes | **Serves:** 2

1 cup frozen cherries, thawed	¼ teaspoon salt
⅓ cup balsamic vinegar	⅛ teaspoon freshly ground black pepper
1 fresh rosemary sprig	1 tablespoon olive oil
1 (8-ounce) pork tenderloin, trimmed of visible fat	

1. Combine the cherries and vinegar in a blender and purée until smooth.
2. Pour into a saucepan, add the rosemary sprig, and bring the mixture to a boil. Reduce the heat to medium-low and simmer for 15 minutes, or until it's reduced by half.
3. While the sauce is simmering, preheat the oven to 425°F and set the rack in the middle position.
4. Season the pork on all sides with the salt and pepper.
5. Heat the oil in a sauté pan over medium-high heat. Add the pork and sear for 3 minutes, turning often, until it's golden on all sides.
6. Transfer the pork to an oven-safe baking dish and roast for 15 minutes, or until the internal temperature is 145°F.
7. Let the pork rest for 5 minutes before serving. Serve sliced and topped with the cherry-balsamic sauce.

Per Serving: Calories: 250; Fat: 8.24g; Sodium: 231mg; Carbs: 16.52g; Fiber: 1.86g; Sugar: 12.85g; Protein: 28.25g

Kofta with Vegetables in Tomato Sauce

Prep Time: 15 minutes | **Cook Time:** 6-8 hours | **Serves:** 4

1 pound raw ground beef	¼ teaspoon ground nutmeg
1 small white or yellow onion, finely diced	¼ teaspoon dried mint
2 garlic cloves, minced	¼ teaspoon paprika
1 tablespoon dried parsley	1 (28-ounce) can no-salt-added diced tomatoes
2 teaspoons ground coriander	2 or 3 zucchini, cut into 1½-inch-thick rounds
1 teaspoon ground cumin	4 ounces mushrooms
½ teaspoon sea salt	1 large red onion, chopped
½ teaspoon freshly ground black pepper	1 green bell pepper, seeded and chopped

1. In a large bowl, mix together the ground beef, white or yellow onion, garlic, parsley, coriander, cumin, salt, pepper, nutmeg, mint, and paprika until well combined and all of the spices and onion are well blended into the meat. Form the meat mixture into 10 to 12 oval patties. Set aside.
2. In a slow cooker, combine the tomatoes, zucchini, mushrooms, red onion, and bell pepper. Stir to mix well.
3. Place the kofta patties on top of the tomato mixture.
4. Cover the cooker and cook for 6 to 8 hours on Low heat.

Per Serving: Calories: 267; Fat: 13.16g; Sodium: 291mg; Carbs: 12.48g; Fiber: 3.38g; Sugar: 7.24g; Protein: 25.05g

Slow-Cooked Moroccan Lamb Roast

Prep Time: 15 minutes | **Cook Time:** 6-8 hours | **Serves:** 6

¼ cup low-sodium beef broth or low-sodium chicken broth	½ teaspoon ground nutmeg
1 teaspoon dried ginger	½ teaspoon ground cloves
1 teaspoon dried cumin	½ teaspoon sea salt
1 teaspoon ground turmeric	½ teaspoon freshly ground black pepper
1 teaspoon paprika	1 (3-pound) lamb roast, trimmed of visible fat
1 teaspoon garlic powder	4 ounces carrots, chopped
1 teaspoon red pepper flakes	¼ cup sliced onion
½ teaspoon ground cinnamon	¼ cup chopped fresh mint
½ teaspoon ground coriander	

1. Pour the broth into a slow cooker.
2. In a small bowl, stir together the ginger, cumin, turmeric, paprika, garlic powder, red pepper flakes, cinnamon, coriander, nutmeg, cloves, salt, and black pepper. Rub the spice mix firmly all over the lamb roast. Put the lamb in the slow cooker and add the carrots and onion.
3. Top everything with the mint.
4. Cover the cooker and cook for 6 to 8 hours on Low heat.

Per Serving: Calories: 348; Fat: 17.18g; Sodium: 294mg; Carbs: 6.57g; Fiber: 1.6g; Sugar: 2.67g; Protein: 40.45g

Moroccan Lamb Shanks and Potatoes

Prep Time: 10 minutes | **Cook Time:** 8 hours | **Serves:** 6

One 15-ounce can crushed tomatoes in purée
3 tablespoons tomato paste
2 tablespoons apricot jam
6 cloves garlic, thinly sliced
3 strips orange zest
¾ teaspoon crushed dried rosemary
½ teaspoon ground ginger
½ teaspoon ground cinnamon
Coarse sea salt
Black pepper
3½ pounds lamb shanks, trimmed of excess fat and cut into 1½-inch slices
1¼ pounds small new potatoes, halved (or quartered, if large)

1. Stir together the tomatoes and purée, tomato paste, jam, garlic, orange zest, rosemary, ginger, and cinnamon in the slow cooker. Season with the salt and pepper.
2. Add the lamb and potatoes, and spoon the tomato mixture over the lamb to coat.
3. Cover and cook until the lamb and potatoes are tender, on low for 8 hours or on high for 5 hours. Season again with the salt and pepper, if desired.
4. Serve hot.

Per Serving: Calories: 408; Fat: 15.22g; Sodium: 252mg; Carbs: 30.54g; Fiber: 3.55g; Sugar: 8.28g; Protein: 34.12g

Grilled Greek–Inspired Beef Kebabs

Prep Time: 15 minutes | **Cook Time:** 15 minutes | **Serves:** 2

6 ounces beef sirloin tip, trimmed of fat and cut into 2-inch pieces
3 cups of any mixture of vegetables: mushrooms, zucchini, summer squash, onions, cherry tomatoes, red peppers
½ cup olive oil
¼ cup freshly squeezed lemon juice
2 tablespoons balsamic vinegar
2 teaspoons dried oregano
1 teaspoon garlic powder
1 teaspoon minced fresh rosemary
1 teaspoon salt

1. Place the meat in a large shallow container or in a plastic freezer bag.
2. Cut the vegetables into similar-size pieces and place them in a second shallow container or freezer bag.
3. For the marinade, combine the olive oil, lemon juice, balsamic vinegar, oregano, garlic powder, rosemary, and salt in a measuring cup. Whisk well to combine. Pour half of the marinade over the meat, and the other half over the vegetables.
4. Place the meat and vegetables in the refrigerator to marinate for 4 hours.
5. When you are ready to cook, preheat the grill to medium-high (350–400°F) and grease the grill grate.
6. Thread the meat onto skewers and the vegetables onto separate skewers.
7. Grill the meat for 3 minutes on each side. They should only take 10 to 12 minutes to cook, but it will depend on how thick the meat is.
8. Grill the vegetables for about 3 minutes on each side or until they have grill marks and are softened.

Per Serving: Calories: 513; Fat: 41g; Sodium: 1138mg; Carbs: 17.75g; Fiber: 4.85g; Sugar: 9.25g; Protein: 26.35g

Chapter 7 Fish and Seafood Recipes

74	**Spicy Barbecued Scallops and Shrimp**
74	**Seared Scallops with Rosemary White Bean Purée**
75	**Roasted Whole Red Snapper with Dill**
75	**Steamed Lemon Salmon**
75	**Grilled Lemon-Garlic Salmon**
76	**Baked Cod with Lemon-Caper Sauce**
76	**Roasted Sea Bass with Root Vegetables**
76	**Mediterranean Baked Salmon with Tomatoes and Olives**
77	**Grilled Halibut with Romesco Sauce**
77	**Moroccan-Spiced Sea Bass**
78	**Lemon-Garlic Roasted Trout**
78	**Roasted Cod with Olives and Artichokes**
78	**Citrus Swordfish with Fresh Herbs**
79	**Dukkah-Spiced Cod with Beet and Arugula Salad**
79	**Steamed Cod with Swiss Chard**
80	**Baked Salmon and Cherry Tomato Pockets**
80	**Air Fryer Herbed Tuna Steaks**
80	**Garlic-Balsamic Shrimp**
81	**Pan-Seared Sea Bass**
81	**Lemon Baked Halibut with Cherry Tomatoes**

Spicy Barbecued Scallops and Shrimp

Prep Time: 15 minutes | **Cook Time:** 1 hour | **Serves:** 4

½ teaspoon paprika	2 cloves garlic, minced
½ teaspoon garlic powder	½ cup olive oil
¼ teaspoon onion powder	¼ cup Worcestershire sauce
¼ teaspoon cayenne pepper	1 tablespoon hot pepper sauce (like tabasco)
¼ teaspoon dried oregano	Juice of 1 lemon
¼ teaspoon dried thyme	1 pound scallops
½ teaspoon sea salt	1 pound large shrimp, unpeeled
½ teaspoon black pepper	1 green onion, finely chopped

1. Combine the paprika, garlic powder, onion powder, cayenne pepper, oregano, thyme, ½ teaspoon salt, and ¼ teaspoon black pepper.
2. Combine the paprika blend, garlic, olive oil, Worcestershire sauce, hot pepper sauce, and lemon juice in the slow cooker. Season with salt and pepper.
3. Cover and cook on high for 30 minutes or until hot.
4. Rinse the scallops and shrimp, and drain.
5. Spoon one-half of the sauce from the slow cooker into a glass measuring cup.
6. Place the scallops and shrimp in the slow cooker with the remaining sauce. Drizzle with the sauce in the measuring cup, and stir to coat.
7. Cover and cook on high for 30 minutes, until the scallops and shrimp are opaque.
8. Turn the heat to warm for serving. Sprinkle with the chopped green onion to serve.

Per Serving: Calories 301; Fat 19.27g; Sodium 684mg; Carbs 5.03g; Fiber 0.93g; Sugar 1.58g; Protein 26.11 g

Seared Scallops with Rosemary White Bean Purée

Prep Time: 15 minutes | **Cook Time:** 15 minutes | **Serves:** 2

4 tablespoons olive oil, divided	½ cup low-sodium chicken stock
2 garlic cloves	Salt
2 teaspoons minced fresh rosemary	Freshly ground black pepper
1 (15-ounce) can white cannellini beans, drained and rinsed	10 ounces sea scallops (about 6)

1. To make the bean purée, heat 2 tablespoons of olive oil in a saucepan over medium-high heat. Add the garlic and sauté for 30 seconds, or just until it's fragrant. Don't let it burn. Add the rosemary and remove the pan from the heat.
2. Add the white beans and chicken stock to the pan, return it to the heat, and stir. Bring the beans to a boil. Reduce the heat to low and simmer for 5 minutes.
3. Transfer the beans to a blender and purée them for 30 seconds, or until they're smooth. Taste and season with salt and pepper. Let them sit in the blender with the lid on to keep them warm while you prepare the scallops.
4. Pat the scallops dry with a paper towel and season them with salt and pepper.
5. Heat the remaining 2 tablespoons of olive oil in a large sauté pan. When the oil is shimmering, add the scallops, flat-side down.
6. Cook the scallops for 2 minutes, or until they're golden on the bottom. Flip them over and cook for another 1 to 2 minutes, or until opaque and slightly firm.
7. To serve, divide the bean purée between two plates and top with the scallops.

Per Serving: Calories 425; Fat 22.2g; Sodium 367mg; Carbs 27.48g; Fiber 5.68g; Sugar 0.89g; Protein 28.47 g

Roasted Whole Red Snapper with Dill

Prep Time: 5 minutes | **Cook Time:** 35 minutes | **Serves:** 4

1 teaspoon salt	dry
½ teaspoon black pepper	2 tablespoons olive oil
½ teaspoon ground cumin	2 garlic cloves, minced
¼ teaspoon cayenne	¼ cup fresh dill
1 (1- to 1½-pound) whole red snapper, cleaned and patted	Lemon wedges, for serving

1. Preheat the air fryer to 360°F
2. In a small bowl, mix together the salt, pepper, cumin, and cayenne.
3. Coat the outside of the fish with olive oil, then sprinkle the seasoning blend over the outside of the fish. Stuff the minced garlic and dill inside the cavity of the fish.
4. Place the snapper into the basket of the air fryer and roast for 20 minutes. Flip the snapper over, and roast for 15 minutes more, or until the snapper reaches an internal temperature of 145°F.

Per Serving: Calories: 242; Fat: 11.63g; Sodium: 668mg; Carbs: 1.75g; Fiber: 0.33g; Sugar: 0.06g; Protein: 32.63g

Steamed Lemon Salmon

Prep Time: 10 minutes | **Cook Time:** 5 minutes | **Serves:** 4

1 lemon, sliced ¼ inch thick	½ teaspoon table salt
4 (6-ounce) skinless salmon fillets, 1½ inches thick	¼ teaspoon pepper

1. Add ½ cup water to the Instant Pot. Fold sheet of aluminum foil into 16 by 6-inch sling. Arrange the lemon slices widthwise in 2 rows across center of sling. Sprinkle the flesh side of salmon with the salt and pepper, then arrange skinned side down on top of lemon slices.
2. Using sling, lower the salmon into the Instant Pot; allow narrow edges of sling to rest along sides of insert. Lock the lid in place and close the pressure release valve. Select high pressure cook function and cook for 3 minutes.
3. Turn off the Instant Pot and quick-release pressure. Carefully remove the lid, allowing the steam to escape away from you. Using sling, transfer the salmon to a large plate. Gently lift and tilt fillets with a spatula to remove the lemon slices. Serve.

Per Serving: Calories: 247; Fat: 10.75g; Sodium: 375mg; Carbs: 2g; Fiber: 0.75g; Sugar: 0.5g; Protein: 34.5g

Grilled Lemon–Garlic Salmon

Prep Time: 5 minutes | **Cook Time:** 10 minutes | **Serves:** 4

1 teaspoon garlic powder	½ teaspoon salt
1 teaspoon onion powder	4 (5- to 6-ounce) salmon fillets with skin on
1 teaspoon freshly ground black pepper	½ cup lemon juice

1. In a small bowl, mix together the garlic powder, black pepper, onion powder, and salt.
2. Put the salmon in a large dish; pour the lemon juice over the salmon.
3. Season the salmon with the seasoning mix.
4. Preheat a grill, grill pan, or lightly oiled skillet to high heat. Place the salmon on the grill or skillet, skin-side down first.
5. Cook each side for 4 minutes. Serve immediately.

Per Serving: Calories: 280; Fat: 11.81g; Sodium: 416mg; Carbs: 2.22g; Fiber: 0.28g; Sugar: 0.55g; Protein: 38.64g

Baked Cod with Lemon-Caper Sauce

Prep Time: 5 minutes | **Cook Time:** 20 minutes | **Serves:** 4

4 (4- to 5-ounce) cod fillets (or any whitefish)	2 tablespoons capers, drained
1 tablespoon extra-virgin olive oil	3 tablespoons lemon juice
1 teaspoon salt, divided	½ teaspoon freshly ground black pepper
4 tablespoons (½ stick) unsalted butter	

1. Preheat the oven to 450°F. Put the cod in a large baking dish and drizzle with the olive oil and ½ teaspoon of salt. Bake for 15 minutes.
2. Right before the fish is done cooking, melt the butter in a small saucepan over medium heat. Add the capers, lemon juice, remaining ½ teaspoon of salt, and pepper; simmer for 30 seconds.
3. Place the fish in a serving dish once it is done baking; spoon the caper sauce over the fish and serve.

Per Serving: Calories: 266; Fat: 18.46g; Sodium: 674mg; Carbs: 2.02g; Fiber: 0.27g; Sugar: 0.29g; Protein: 22.74g

Roasted Sea Bass with Root Vegetables

Prep Time: 10 minutes | **Cook Time:** 15 minutes | **Serves:** 4

1 carrot, diced small	4 sea bass fillets
1 parsnip, diced small	½ teaspoon onion powder
1 rutabaga, diced small	2 garlic cloves, minced
¼ cup olive oil	1 lemon, sliced, plus additional wedges for serving
2 teaspoons salt, divided	

1. Preheat the air fryer to 380°F.
2. In a small bowl, toss the carrot, parsnip, and rutabaga with olive oil and 1 teaspoon salt.
3. Lightly season the sea bass with the remaining 1 teaspoon of salt and the onion powder, then place it into the air fryer basket in a single layer.
4. Spread the garlic over the top of each fillet, then cover with lemon slices.
5. Pour the prepared vegetables into the basket around and on top of the fish. Roast for 15 minutes.
6. Serve with additional lemon wedges if desired.

Per Serving: Calories: 360; Fat: 18.88g; Sodium: 1271mg; Carbs: 11.38g; Fiber: 3.08g; Sugar: 3.13g; Protein: 36.75g

Mediterranean Baked Salmon with Tomatoes and Olives

Prep Time: 5 minutes | **Cook Time:** 8 minutes | **Serves:** 4

2 tablespoons olive oil	1 teaspoon chopped fresh dill
4 (1½-inch-thick) salmon fillets	2 Roma tomatoes, diced
½ teaspoon salt	¼ cup sliced Kalamata olives
¼ teaspoon cayenne	4 lemon slices

1. Preheat the air fryer to 380°F.
2. Brush the olive oil on both sides of the salmon fillets, and then season them lightly with salt, cayenne, and dill.
3. Place the fillets in a single layer in the basket of the air fryer, then layer the tomatoes and olives over the top. Top each fillet with a lemon slice.
4. Bake for 8 minutes, or until the salmon has reached an internal temperature of 145°F.

Per Serving: Calories 283; Fat 18.77g; Sodium 402mg; Carbs 3.11g; Fiber 0.81g; Sugar 0.97g; Protein 24.13g

Grilled Halibut with Romesco Sauce

Prep Time: 20 minutes | **Cook Time:** 10 minutes | **Serves:** 2

For the Romesco Sauce:
½ cup jarred roasted piquillo peppers
2 tablespoons sun-dried tomatoes in olive oil with herbs
2 small garlic cloves
¼ cup raw, unsalted almonds
2 tablespoons red wine vinegar
Pinch salt
¼ teaspoon smoked paprika (or more to taste)
¼ cup olive oil
1 to 2 tablespoons water

For the Halibut:
2 (5-ounce) halibut steaks
1 tablespoon olive oil
Salt
Freshly ground black pepper

To make the romesco sauce:
1. Combine the piquillo peppers, sun-dried tomatoes, garlic, almonds, vinegar, salt, and paprika in a food processor or a blender and blend until mostly smooth. While the mixture is blending, drizzle in the olive oil.
2. Taste and adjust seasonings. If you prefer a smoother sauce, add water, 1 tablespoon at a time, until sauce reaches your desired consistency.

To make the salmon:
1. Heat the grill to medium-high (350–400°F) and oil the grill grates.
2. Brush the fish with olive oil, and season with salt and pepper.
3. When the grill is hot, grill the fish for about 5 minutes per side, or until it's opaque and flakes easily. Serve topped with a few tablespoons of the romesco sauce.
4. Store any remaining sauce in an airtight container in the refrigerator for up to a week.

Per Serving: Calories 445; Fat 34.18g; Sodium 341mg; Carbs 11.29g; Fiber 2.89g; Sugar 3.67g; Protein 26.46 g

Moroccan–Spiced Sea Bass

Prep Time: 15 minutes | **Cook Time:** 2 hours | **Serves:** 8

2 tablespoons extra-virgin olive oil
1 large yellow onion, finely chopped
1 medium red bell pepper, cut into ½-inch strips
1 medium yellow bell pepper, cut into ½-inch strips
4 garlic cloves, minced
1 teaspoon saffron threads, crushed in the palm of your hand
1½ teaspoons sweet paprika
¼ teaspoon hot paprika or ¼ teaspoon smoked paprika (or pimentón)
½ teaspoon ground ginger
One 15-ounce can diced tomatoes, with the juice
¼ cup fresh orange juice
2 pounds fresh sea bass fillets
¼ cup finely chopped fresh flat-leaf parsley
¼ cup finely chopped fresh cilantro
Sea salt
Black pepper
1 navel orange, thinly sliced, for garnish

1. In a large skillet, heat the olive oil over medium-high heat. Add the onion, red and yellow bell peppers, garlic, saffron, sweet paprika, hot or smoked paprika, and ginger and cook, stirring often, for 3 minutes, or until the onion begins to soften.
2. Add the tomatoes and stir for another 2 minutes, to blend the flavors.
3. Transfer the mixture to the slow cooker and stir in the orange juice.
4. Place the sea bass fillets on top of the tomato mixture, and spoon some of the mixture over the fish. Cover and cook on high for 2 hours, or on low for 3 to 4 hours. At the end of the cooking time, the sea bass should be opaque in the center.
5. Carefully lift the fish out of the slow cooker with a spatula and transfer to a serving platter. Cover loosely with aluminum foil.
6. Skim off any excess fat from the sauce, stir in the parsley and cilantro, and season with salt and pepper.
7. Spoon some of the sauce over the fish, and garnish with the orange slices. Serve hot, passing the remaining sauce on the side.

Per Serving: Calories: 199; Fat: 6.88g; Sodium: 147mg; Carbs: 8.67g; Fiber: 1.83g; Sugar: 4.43g; Protein: 24.23g

Lemon–Garlic Roasted Trout

Prep Time: 5 minutes | **Cook Time:** 15 minutes | **Serves:** 4

4 trout fillets	1 teaspoon black pepper
2 tablespoons olive oil	2 garlic cloves, sliced
½ teaspoon salt	1 lemon, sliced, plus additional wedges for serving

1. Preheat the air fryer to 380°F.
2. Brush each fillet with the olive oil on both sides and season with the salt and pepper. Arrange the fillets in an even layer in the air fryer basket.
3. Place the sliced garlic over the tops of the trout fillets, then top the garlic with lemon slices and roast for 12 to 15 minutes, or until it has reached an internal temperature of 145°F.
4. Serve with the fresh lemon wedges.

Per Serving: Calories: 251; Fat: 13.5g; Sodium: 424mg; Carbs: 3.88g; Fiber: 0.96g; Sugar: 0.51g; Protein: 27.63g

Roasted Cod with Olives and Artichokes

Prep Time: 10 minutes | **Cook Time:** 20 minutes | **Serves:** 2

1 tablespoon olive oil	halved
½ medium onion, minced	¼ cup pitted Greek olives, drained
2 garlic cloves, minced	10 ounces wild cod (2 smaller pieces may fit better in the pan)
1 teaspoon oregano	
1 (15-ounce) can diced tomatoes with basil	Salt
1 (15-ounce) can artichoke hearts in water, drained and	Freshly ground black pepper

1. Heat the olive oil in a sauté pan over medium-high heat. Add the onion and sauté for about 10 minutes, or until golden. Add the garlic and oregano and cook for another 30 seconds.
2. Mix in the tomatoes, artichoke hearts, and olives.
3. Place the cod on top of the vegetables. Cover the pan and cook for 10 minutes, or until the fish is opaque and flakes apart easily. Season with the salt and pepper.

Per Serving: Calories 314; Fat 11.36g; Sodium 748mg; Carbs 20.25g; Fiber 4.53g; Sugar 6.15g; Protein 34.79 g

Citrus Swordfish with Fresh Herbs

Prep Time: 10 minutes | **Cook Time:** 1½ hours | **Serves:** 4

Nonstick cooking oil spray	1 tablespoon olive oil
1½ pounds swordfish fillets	2 teaspoons lemon zest
Sea salt	2 teaspoons orange zest
Black pepper	Orange and lemon slices, for garnish
1 yellow onion, chopped	Fresh parsley sprigs, for garnish
5 tablespoons chopped fresh flat-leaf parsley	

1. Coat the interior of the slow cooker crock with nonstick cooking oil spray.
2. Season the fish fillets with salt and pepper. Place the fish in the slow cooker.
3. Distribute the onion, parsley, olive oil, lemon zest, and orange zest over fish.
4. Cover and cook on low for 1½ hours.
5. Serve hot, garnished with the orange and lemon slices and sprigs of fresh parsley.

Per Serving: Calories 245; Fat 9.68g; Sodium 97mg; Carbs 6.14g; Fiber 1.36g; Sugar 3.89g; Protein 31.47 g

Dukkah-Spiced Cod with Beet and Arugula Salad

Prep Time: 15 minutes | Cook Time: 8 minutes | Serves: 4

¼ cup extra-virgin olive oil, divided, plus extra for drizzling	1 tablespoon dukkah, plus extra for sprinkling
1 shallot, sliced thin	¼ teaspoon table salt
2 garlic cloves, minced	4 (6-ounce) skinless cod fillets, 1½ inches thick
1½ pounds small beets, scrubbed, trimmed, and cut into ½-inch wedges	1 tablespoon lemon juice
½ cup chicken or vegetable broth	2 ounces (2 cups) baby arugula

1. Using the highest sauté function, heat 1 tablespoon oil in the Instant Pot until shimmering. Add the shallot and cook until softened, about 2 minutes. Stir in the garlic and cook until fragrant, about 30 seconds. Stir in the beets and broth. Lock the lid in place and close the pressure release valve. Select high pressure cook function and cook for 3 minutes. Turn off the Instant Pot and quick-release pressure. Carefully remove the lid, allowing the steam to escape away from you.
2. Fold sheet of aluminum foil into 16 by 6-inch sling. Combine 2 tablespoons oil, dukkah, and salt in a bowl, then brush the cod with oil mixture. Arrange the cod skinned side down in center of sling. Using sling, lower the cod into the Instant Pot; allow narrow edges of sling to rest along sides of insert. Lock the lid in place and close the pressure release valve. Select high pressure cook function and cook for 2 minutes.
3. Turn off the Instant Pot and quick-release pressure. Carefully remove the lid, allowing the steam to escape away from you. Using sling, transfer the cod to a large plate. Tent with foil and let rest while finishing beet salad.
4. Combine the lemon juice and remaining 1 tablespoon oil in a large bowl. Using a slotted spoon, transfer the beets to the bowl with oil mixture. Add the arugula and gently toss to combine. Season with the salt and pepper to taste. Serve the cod with salad, sprinkling individual portions with extra dukkah and drizzling with the extra oil.

Per Serving: Calories: 316; Fat: 15.71g; Sodium: 313mg; Carbs: 14.96g; Fiber: 2.48g; Sugar: 8.15g; Protein: 29.21g

Steamed Cod with Swiss Chard

Prep Time: 5 minutes | Cook Time: 12 minutes | Serves: 4

1 teaspoon salt	½ white onion, thinly sliced
½ teaspoon dried oregano	2 cups Swiss chard, washed, stemmed, and torn into pieces
½ teaspoon dried thyme	¼ cup olive oil
½ teaspoon garlic powder	1 lemon, quartered
4 cod fillets	

1. Preheat the air fryer to 380°F.
2. In a small bowl, whisk together the salt, oregano, thyme, and garlic powder.
3. Tear off four pieces of aluminum foil, with each sheet being large enough to envelop one cod fillet and a quarter of the vegetables.
4. Place a cod fillet in the middle of each sheet of foil, then sprinkle on all sides with the spice mixture.
5. In each foil packet, place a quarter of the onion slices and ½ cup Swiss chard, then drizzle 1 tablespoon olive oil and squeeze ¼ lemon over the contents of each foil packet.
6. Fold and seal the sides of the foil packets and then place them into the air fryer basket. Steam for 12 minutes.
7. Remove from the basket, and carefully open each packet to avoid a steam burn.

Per Serving: Calories: 246; Fat: 14.75g; Sodium: 661mg; Carbs: 6.25g; Fiber: 1.63g; Sugar: 1.38g; Protein: 22.75g

Baked Salmon and Cherry Tomato Pockets

Prep Time: 5 minutes | **Cook Time:** 25 minutes | **Serves:** 4

1 pint (2 cups) cherry tomatoes	3 tablespoons unsalted butter, melted
3 tablespoons extra-virgin olive oil	½ teaspoon salt
3 tablespoons lemon juice	4 (5-ounce) salmon fillets
1 teaspoon oregano	

1. Preheat the oven to 400°F.
2. Cut the tomatoes in half and put them in a bowl.
3. Add the olive oil, lemon juice, oregano, melted butter, and salt to the tomatoes and toss to combine.
4. Cut 4 pieces of foil, about 12-by-12 inches each.
5. Place the salmon in the middle of each piece of foil.
6. Divide the tomato mixture evenly over the 4 pieces of salmon. Bring the ends of the foil together and seal to form a closed pocket.
7. Place the 4 pockets on a baking sheet. Cook for 25 minutes.
8. To serve, place each pocket on a plate and let your guests open to reveal the baked salmon and tomatoes.

Per Serving: Calories: 337; Fat: 21.12g; Sodium: 274mg; Carbs: 3.35g; Fiber: 0.83g; Sugar: 1.42g; Protein: 31.96g

Air Fryer Herbed Tuna Steaks

Prep Time: 5 minutes | **Cook Time:** 9 minutes | **Serves:** 4

1 teaspoon garlic powder	4 tuna steaks
½ teaspoon salt	2 tablespoons olive oil
¼ teaspoon dried thyme	1 lemon, quartered
¼ teaspoon dried oregano	

1. Preheat the air fryer to 380°F.
2. In a small bowl, whisk together the garlic powder, salt, thyme, and oregano.
3. Coat the tuna steaks with olive oil. Season both sides of each steak with the seasoning blend. Place the steaks in a single layer in the air fryer basket.
4. Roast for 5 minutes, then flip and roast for another 3 to 4 minutes.

Per Serving: Calories: 210; Fat: 10.36g; Sodium: 268mg; Carbs: 2.11g; Fiber: 0.87g; Sugar: 0.58g; Protein: 27.46g

Garlic–Balsamic Shrimp

Prep Time: 5 minutes | **Cook Time:** 8 minutes | **Serves:** 4

½ cup olive oil	¼ teaspoon salt
4 garlic cloves, minced	1 Roma tomato, diced
1 tablespoon balsamic vinegar	¼ cup Kalamata olives
¼ teaspoon cayenne pepper	1 pound medium shrimp, cleaned and deveined

1. Preheat the air fryer to 380°F.
2. In a small bowl, combine the olive oil, garlic, balsamic, cayenne, and salt.
3. Divide the tomatoes and olives among four small ramekins. Then divide shrimp among the ramekins, and pour a quarter of the oil mixture over the shrimp.
4. Roast for 6 to 8 minutes, or until the shrimp are cooked through.

Per Serving: Calories: 317.25; Fat: 19.56g; Sodium: 687.75mg; Carbs: 4.74g; Fiber: 1.07g; Sugar: 1.11g; Protein: 28.26g

Pan-Seared Sea Bass

Prep Time: 5 minutes | **Cook Time:** 10 minutes | **Serves:** 4

4 (5-ounce) sea bass fillets
½ teaspoon salt
1 tablespoon smoked paprika
3 tablespoons unsalted butter
Lemon wedges

1. Season the fish on both sides with the salt. Repeat with the paprika.
2. Preheat a skillet over high heat. Melt the butter.
3. Once the butter is melted, add the fish and cook for 4 minutes on each side.
4. Once the fish is done cooking, move to a serving dish and squeeze the lemon over the top.

Per Serving: Calories: 215; Fat: 12.77g; Sodium: 366mg; Carbs: 1.35g; Fiber: 0.18g; Sugar: 0g; Protein: 23.48g

Lemon Baked Halibut with Cherry Tomatoes

Prep Time: 5 minutes | **Cook Time:** 15 minutes | **Serves:** 4

4 (5-ounce) pieces of boneless halibut, skin on
1 pint (2 cups) cherry tomatoes
3 tablespoons garlic, minced
½ cup lemon juice
¼ cup extra-virgin olive oil
1 teaspoon salt

1. Preheat the oven to 425°F.
2. Put the halibut in a large baking dish; place the tomatoes around the halibut.
3. In a small bowl, combine the garlic, lemon juice, olive oil, and salt.
4. Pour the sauce over the halibut and tomatoes. Place the baking dish in the oven and bake for 15 minutes. Serve immediately.

Per Serving: Calories: 272; Fat: 14.43g; Sodium: 646mg; Carbs: 7.98g; Fiber: 1.5g; Sugar: 3.83g; Protein: 26.13g

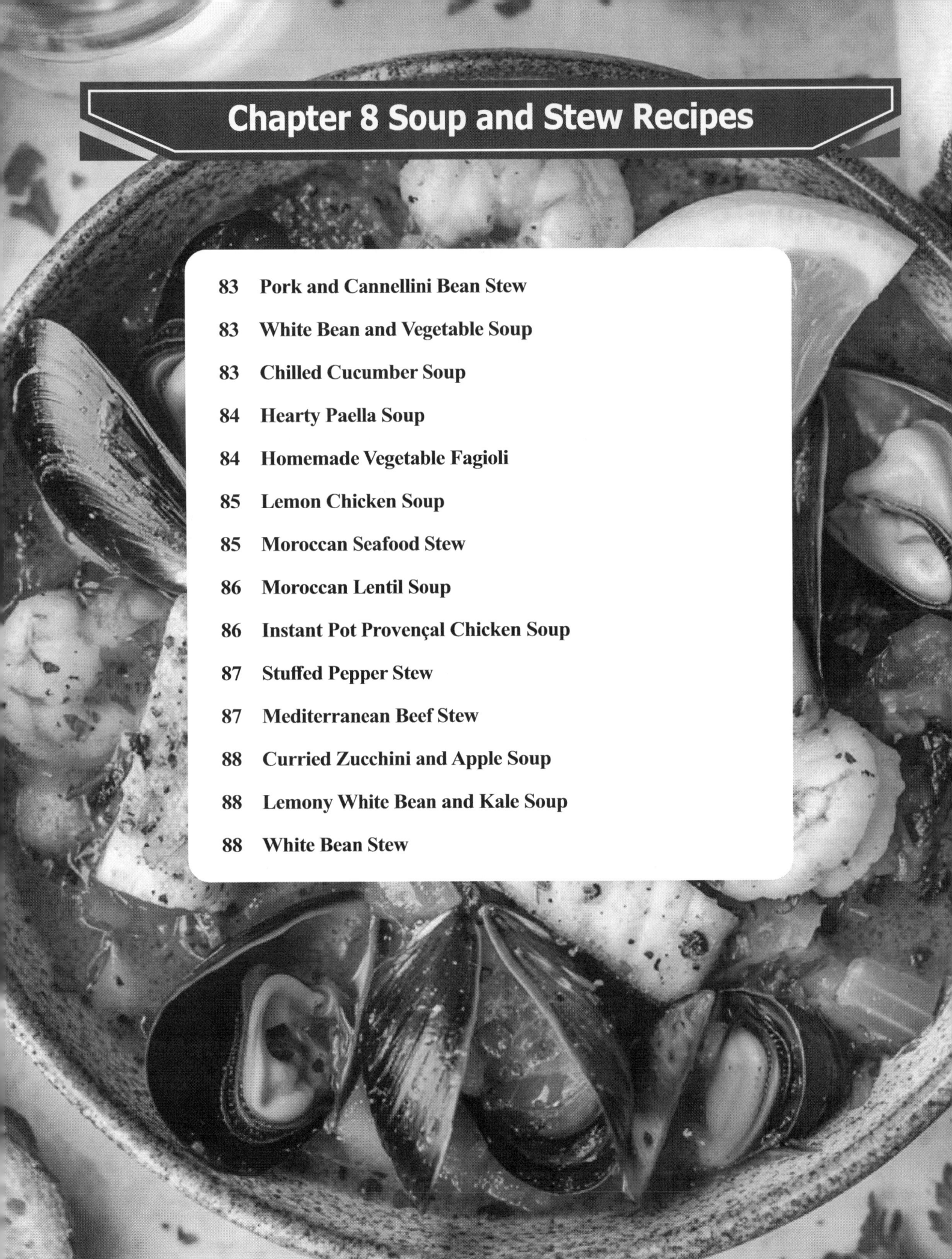

Chapter 8 Soup and Stew Recipes

83 Pork and Cannellini Bean Stew

83 White Bean and Vegetable Soup

83 Chilled Cucumber Soup

84 Hearty Paella Soup

84 Homemade Vegetable Fagioli

85 Lemon Chicken Soup

85 Moroccan Seafood Stew

86 Moroccan Lentil Soup

86 Instant Pot Provençal Chicken Soup

87 Stuffed Pepper Stew

87 Mediterranean Beef Stew

88 Curried Zucchini and Apple Soup

88 Lemony White Bean and Kale Soup

88 White Bean Stew

Pork and Cannellini Bean Stew

Prep Time: 15 minutes | **Cook Time:** 1 hour | **Serves:** 6

1 cup dried cannellini beans
¼ cup olive oil
1 medium onion, diced
2 pounds pork roast, cut into 1-inch chunks
3 cups water
1 (8-ounce) can tomato paste
¼ cup flat-leaf parsley, chopped
½ teaspoon dried thyme
Sea salt and freshly ground pepper, to taste

1. Rinse and sort the beans.
2. Cover the beans with water, and allow to soak overnight. Heat the olive oil in a large stew pot.
3. Add the onion, stirring occasionally, until golden brown.
4. Add the pork chunks and cook 5–8 minutes, stirring frequently, until the pork is browned.
5. Drain and rinse the beans, and add to the pot.
6. Add the water, and bring to a boil. Reduce the heat and simmer for 45 minutes, until beans are tender.
7. Add the tomato paste, parsley, and thyme, and simmer for an additional 15 minutes, or until the sauce thickens slightly. Season to taste.

Per Serving: Calories 320; Fat 12.5g; Sodium 340mg; Carbs 19.7g; Fiber 4.2g; Sugar 4.1g; Protein 29.8g

White Bean and Vegetable Soup

Prep Time: 10 minutes | **Cook Time:** 25 minutes | **Serves:** 6

3 tablespoons extra-virgin olive oil
1 large onion, finely chopped
3 large garlic cloves, minced
2 cups carrots, diced
2 cups celery, diced
2 (15-ounce) cans white beans, rinsed and drained
8 cups vegetable broth
1 teaspoon salt
½ teaspoon freshly ground black pepper

1. In a large pot over medium heat, cook the olive oil, onion, and garlic for 2 to 3 minutes.
2. Add the carrots and celery, and cook for an additional 3 to 5 minutes, stirring occasionally.
3. Add the beans, broth, salt, and pepper. Stir and let simmer for 15 to 17 minutes, stirring occasionally. Serve warm.

Per Serving: Calories 194; Fat 5.23g; Sodium 614mg; Carbs 27.46g; Fiber 6.95g; Sugar 5.48g; Protein 7.86g

Chilled Cucumber Soup

Prep Time: 10 minutes | **Cook Time:** 0 minutes | **Serves:** 4

2 seedless cucumbers, peeled and cut into chunks
2 cups plain Greek yogurt
½ cup mint, finely chopped
2 garlic cloves, minced
2 cups chicken broth or vegetable stock
3 teaspoons fresh dill
1 tablespoon tomato paste
Sea salt and freshly ground pepper, to taste

1. Puree the cucumber, yogurt, mint, and garlic in a food processor or blender.
2. Add the chicken broth, dill, tomato paste, sea salt, and pepper, and blend completely.
3. Refrigerate for at least 2 hours before serving.

Per Serving: Calories 120; Fat 3.6g; Sodium 310mg; Carbs 12.70g; Fiber 1.20g; Sugar 6g; Protein 10.2g

Hearty Paella Soup

Prep Time: 5 minutes | Cook time: 25 minutes | **Serves:** 6

1 cup frozen green peas	1 teaspoon dried thyme
2 tablespoons extra-virgin olive oil	2 teaspoons smoked paprika
1 cup chopped onion (about ½ medium onion)	2½ cups uncooked instant brown rice
1½ cups coarsely chopped red bell pepper (about 1 large pepper)	2 cups low-sodium or no-salt-added chicken broth
	2½ cups water
1½ cups coarsely chopped green bell pepper (about 1 large pepper)	1 (28-ounce) can low-sodium or no-salt-added crushed tomatoes
2 garlic cloves, chopped (about 1 teaspoon)	1 pound fresh raw medium shrimp (or frozen raw shrimp completely thawed), shells and tails removed
1 teaspoon ground turmeric	

1. Put the frozen peas on the counter to partially thaw as the soup is being prepared.
2. In a large stockpot over medium-high heat, heat the oil. Add the onion, red bell pepper, and green bell peppers, and garlic. Cook for 8 minutes, stirring occasionally. Add the turmeric, thyme, and smoked paprika, and cook for 2 minutes more, stirring often. Stir in the rice, broth, and water. Bring to a boil over high heat. Cover, reduce the heat to medium-low, and cook for 10 minutes.
3. Stir the peas, tomatoes, and shrimp into the soup. Cook for 4 to 6 minutes, until the shrimp is cooked, turning from gray to pink and white. The soup will be very thick, almost like stew, when ready to serve.

Per Serving: Calories 303; Fat 5.94g; Sodium 488mg; Carbs 47.37g; Fiber 4.21g; Sugar 6.13g; Protein 17.58 g

Homemade Vegetable Fagioli

Prep Time: 30 minutes | **Cook Time:** 60 minutes | **Serves:** 2

1 tablespoon olive oil	1 cup packed kale, stemmed and chopped
2 medium carrots, diced (about ¾ cup)	1 (15-ounce) can red kidney beans, drained and rinsed
2 medium celery stalks, diced (about ½ cup)	1 (15-ounce) can cannellini beans, drained and rinsed
½ medium onion, diced (about ¾ cup)	½ cup fresh basil, chopped
1 large garlic clove, minced	Salt
3 tablespoons tomato paste	Freshly ground black pepper
4 cups low-sodium vegetable broth	

1. Heat the olive oil in a stockpot over medium-high heat. Add the carrots, celery, onion, and garlic and sauté for 10 minutes, or until the vegetables start to turn golden.
2. Stir in the tomato paste and cook for about 30 seconds.
3. Add the vegetable broth and bring the soup to a boil. Cover, and reduce the heat to low. Cook the soup for 45 minutes, or until the carrots are tender.
4. Using an immersion blender, purée the soup so that it's partly smooth, but with some chunks of vegetables. If you don't have an immersion blender, scoop out about ⅓ of the soup and blend it in a blender, then add it back to the pot.
5. Add the kale, beans, and basil. Season with the salt and pepper.

Per Serving: Calories 330; Fat 6.40g; Sodium 600mg; Carbs 55.2g; Fiber 15.3g; Sugar 11.20g; Protein 14.8g

Lemon Chicken Soup

Prep Time: 15 minutes | **Cook Time:** 60 minutes | **Serves:** 2

½ large onion	1½ cups (about 5 ounces) shredded rotisserie chicken
2 medium carrots	3 tablespoons freshly squeezed lemon juice
1 celery stalk	1 egg yolk
1 garlic clove	2 tablespoons chopped fresh dill
5 cups low-sodium chicken stock	2 tablespoons chopped fresh parsley
¼ cup brown rice	Salt

1. Place the onion, carrots, celery, and garlic in a food processor fitted with the chopping blade and pulse it until the vegetables are minced. You can also mince them by hand.
2. Add the vegetables and chicken stock to a stockpot or Dutch oven and bring it to a boil over high heat.
3. Reduce the heat to medium-low and add the rice, shredded chicken and lemon juice. Cover, and allow the soup to simmer for 40 minutes, or until the rice is cooked.
4. In a small bowl, whisk the egg yolk lightly. Very slowly, while whisking with one hand, pour about ½ of a ladle of the broth into the egg yolk to warm, or temper, the yolk. Slowly add another ladle of broth and continue to whisk. Do not skip this step (see Prep Tip).
5. Remove the soup from the heat and pour the whisked egg yolk–broth mixture into the pot. Stir well to combine.
6. Add the fresh dill and parsley. Season with salt, and serve.
7. If you want to reheat any leftovers, heat it very slowly and don't let the soup come to a full boil.

Per Serving: Calories 330; Fat 6.40g; Sodium 600mg; Carbs 55.2g; Fiber 15.3g; Sugar 11.2g; Protein 14.8g

Moroccan Seafood Stew

Prep Time: 20 minutes | **Cook Time:** 2 hours | **Serves:** 8

2 tablespoons extra-virgin olive oil	One 15-ounce can diced tomatoes, with the juice
1 large yellow onion, finely chopped	¼ cup fresh orange juice
1 medium red bell pepper, cut into ½-inch strips	2 pounds skinless sea bass fillets
1 medium yellow bell pepper, cut into ½-inch strips	¼ cup finely chopped fresh flat-leaf parsley
4 garlic cloves, minced	¼ cup finely chopped fresh cilantro
1 teaspoon saffron threads, crushed in the palm of your hand	Sea salt
1½ teaspoons sweet paprika	Black pepper
¼ teaspoon hot paprika	1 navel orange, thinly sliced, for garnish
½ teaspoon ground ginger	

1. In a large skillet, heat the olive oil over medium-high heat. Sauté the onion, bell peppers, and garlic. Add the saffron, sweet paprika, hot paprika, and ginger. Cook for 3 minutes, or until the onion begins to soften.
2. Add the tomatoes and sauté for another 2 minutes, to blend the flavors.
3. Transfer the mixture to the slow cooker and stir in the orange juice. Place the sea bass on top of the tomato mixture, and spoon some of the mixture over the fish. Cover and cook on high for 2 hours or on low 3 to 4 hours.
4. At the end of the cooking time, the sea bass should be opaque in the center.
5. Using a fish spatula or any thin spatula, carefully lift the fish out of the slow cooker, transfer it to a serving platter, and cover it loosely with aluminum foil.
6. Skim off any excess fat from the sauce, stir in the parsley and cilantro, and season with salt and pepper.
7. Spoon some of the sauce over the fish, and garnish with the orange slices. Serve hot, passing the remaining sauce on the side.

Per Serving: Calories 183; Fat 5.83g; Sodium 245mg; Carbs 10.12g; Fiber 2.03g; Sugar 4.69g; Protein 24.28g

Moroccan Lentil Soup

Prep Time: 10 minutes | **Cook Time:** 4 to 5 hours | **Serves:** 6

1 cup chopped onions	4 cups low-sodium vegetable stock
1 cup chopped carrots	1½ cups chopped cauliflower
3 cloves garlic, minced	1 cup dry lentils
1 teaspoon extra-virgin olive oil	One 28-ounce can diced tomatoes, with the juice
1 teaspoon ground cumin	1 tablespoon tomato paste
½ teaspoon ground coriander	1 cup gently packed chopped fresh spinach
1 teaspoon ground turmeric	¼ cup chopped fresh cilantro
¼ teaspoon ground cinnamon	1 tablespoon red wine vinegar, plus more for serving (optional)
¼ teaspoon freshly ground black pepper	

1. Combine the onions, carrots, garlic, olive oil, cumin, coriander, turmeric, cinnamon, and ¼ teaspoon black pepper in the slow cooker.
2. Add the vegetable stock, cauliflower, lentils, tomatoes, and tomato paste and stir to combine.
3. Cover and cook on high for 4 to 5 hours or on low for 8 to 10 hours, until the lentils are tender.
4. During the last 30 minutes of cooking, stir in the spinach.
5. Just before serving, stir in the cilantro and vinegar. Serve hot with more vinegar, if desired.

Per Serving: Calories 163; Fat 1.95g; Sodium 390mg; Carbs 29.58g; Fiber 9.21g; Sugar 7.32g; Protein 8.12g

Instant Pot Provençal Chicken Soup

Prep Time: 20 minutes | **Cook Time:** 30 minutes | **Serves:** 6-8

1 tablespoon extra-virgin olive oil	2 anchovy fillets, minced
2 fennel bulbs, 2 tablespoons fronds minced, stalks discarded, bulbs halved, cored, and cut into ½-inch pieces	7 cups water, divided
	1 (14.5-ounce) can diced tomatoes, drained
1 onion, chopped	2 carrots, peeled, halved lengthwise, and sliced ½ inch thick
1¾ teaspoons table salt	2 (12-ounce) bone-in split chicken breasts, trimmed
2 tablespoons tomato paste	4 (5- to 7-ounce) bone-in chicken thighs, trimmed
4 garlic cloves, minced	½ cup pitted brine-cured green olives, chopped
1 tablespoon minced fresh thyme or 1 teaspoon dried	1 teaspoon grated orange zest

1. Using the highest sauté function, heat oil in the Instant Pot until shimmering. Add fennel pieces, onion, and salt and cook until vegetables are softened, about 5 minutes. Stir in tomato paste, garlic, thyme, and anchovies and cook until fragrant, about 30 seconds. Stir in 5 cups water, scraping up any browned bits, then stir in tomatoes and carrots. Nestle chicken breasts and thighs in pot.
2. Lock the lid in place and close the pressure release valve. Select high pressure cook function and cook for 20 minutes. Turn off the Instant Pot and quick-release pressure. Carefully remove the lid, allowing the steam to escape away from you.
3. Transfer chicken to cutting board, let cool slightly, then shred into bite-size pieces using 2 forks; discard skin and bones.
4. Using wide, shallow spoon, skim excess fat from surface of soup. Stir chicken and any accumulated juices, olives, and remaining 2 cups water into soup and allow to sit until heated through, about 3 minutes. Stir in fennel fronds and orange zest, and season with salt and pepper to taste. Serve.

Per Serving: Calories 210; Fat 7.2g; Sodium 750mg; Carbs 10.35g; Fiber 2.25g; Sugar 4.10g; Protein 25.80g

Stuffed Pepper Stew

Prep Time: 20 minutes | **Cook Time:** 50 minutes | **Serves:** 2

2 tablespoons olive oil	1 cup low-sodium vegetable stock
2 sweet peppers, diced (about 2 cups)	1 cup low-sodium tomato juice
½ large onion, minced	¼ cup brown lentils
1 garlic clove, minced	¼ cup brown rice
1 teaspoon oregano	Salt
1 tablespoon gluten-free vegetarian Worcestershire sauce	

1. Heat olive oil in a Dutch oven over medium-high heat. Add the sweet peppers and onion and sauté for 10 minutes, or until the peppers are wilted and the onion starts to turn golden.
2. Add the garlic, oregano, and Worcestershire sauce, and cook for another 30 seconds. Add the vegetable stock, tomato juice, lentils, and rice.
3. Bring the mixture to a boil. Cover, and reduce the heat to medium-low. Simmer for 45 minutes, or until the rice is cooked and the lentils are softened. Season with the salt.

Per Serving: Calories 285; Fat 10g; Sodium 310mg; Carbs 40.5g; Fiber 7.8g; Sugar 9.2g; Protein 7.1g

Mediterranean Beef Stew

Prep Time: 15 minutes | **Cook Time:** 8⅓ hours | **Serves:** 6

8 ounces mushrooms, sliced	½ cup thinly sliced garlic cloves
1 large yellow onion, diced	2 tablespoons finely chopped fresh rosemary (or 1 tablespoon dried rosemary)
2 tablespoons olive oil	
2 pounds chuck steak, trimmed and cut into bite-size pieces	2 tablespoons finely chopped fresh flat-leaf parsley (or 1 tablespoon dried parsley)
1 cup beef stock	
One 15-ounce can diced tomatoes, with the juice	2 tablespoons capers, drained
½ cup (4 ounces) tomato sauce	Sea salt
¼ cup balsamic vinegar	Black pepper
One 5-ounce can chopped black olives	

1. Place the mushrooms and onion in the slow cooker.
2. Heat the olive oil in a large skillet over medium-high heat. Add the beef and cook until well browned, stirring often, for 10 to 15 minutes. Don't rush the browning step, and decrease the heat to medium if the beef browns too quickly. Add the beef to the slow cooker.
3. Add the beef stock to the skillet and simmer for 5 minutes or until slightly reduced, scraping up the flavorful brown bits from the bottom of the pan with a wooden spoon. Add the stock to the slow cooker.
4. Add the diced tomatoes, tomato sauce, vinegar, olives, garlic, rosemary, parsley, and capers to the slow cooker. Season with salt and pepper. Stir gently to combine. Cover and cook on low for 6 to 8 hours. (It is possible to cook on high for 3 to 4 hours, but the lower setting yields the best results.) Season with additional salt and pepper, if desired, and serve hot.

Per Serving: Calories 285; Fat 12.67g; Sodium 454mg; Carbs 11.15g; Fiber 2.12g; Sugar 4.71g; Protein 30.48g

Curried Zucchini and Apple Soup

Prep Time: 10 minutes | **Cook Time:** 20 minutes | **Serves:** 4-6

¼ cup extra-virgin olive oil
1 medium onion, chopped (about ½ cup)
1 carrot, shredded
1 small garlic clove, minced
4 cups low-sodium chicken broth

2 medium zucchini, thinly sliced
2 apples, peeled and chopped
2½ teaspoons curry powder
¼ teaspoon salt

1. In a large pot, heat the oil over medium heat. Sauté the onion, carrot, and garlic and cook until tender. Add the chicken broth, zucchini, apples, and curry powder.
2. Boil for 2 minutes, reduce the heat, and simmer for 20 minutes, until the vegetables are tender.
3. Season with the salt and serve.

Per Serving: Calories 123; Fat 7.37g; Sodium 273mg; Carbs 14.33g; Fiber 2.26g; Sugar 8.5g; Protein 2.47g

Lemony White Bean and Kale Soup

Prep Time: 25 minutes | **Cook Time:** 30 minutes | **Serves:** 4

1 to 2 tablespoons extra-virgin olive oil
1 large shallot, minced
1 large purple carrot, chopped
1 celery stalk, chopped
1 teaspoon garlic powder
3 cups low-sodium vegetable broth
1 (15-ounce) can cannellini beans

1 cup chopped baby kale
1 teaspoon salt (optional)
½ teaspoon freshly ground black pepper (optional)
1 lemon, juiced and zested
1½ tablespoons chopped fresh thyme (optional)
3 tablespoons chopped fresh oregano (optional)

1. In a large, deep pot, heat the oil. Add the shallot, carrot, celery, and garlic powder and sauté on medium-low heat for 3 to 5 minutes, until the vegetables are golden.
2. Add the vegetable broth and beans and bring to a simmer. Cook for 15 minutes.
3. Add in the kale, salt (if using), and pepper (if using). Cook for another 5 to 10 minutes, until the kale is soft. Right before serving, stir in the lemon juice and zest, thyme (if using), and oregano (if using).

Per Serving: Calories 138; Fat 5.35g; Sodium 421mg; Carbs 20.56g; Fiber 5.13g; Sugar 3.75g; Protein 5.82g

White Bean Stew

Prep time: 10 minutes | **Cook Time:** 30 minutes | **Serves:** 4-6

3 tablespoons extra-virgin olive oil
1 large onion, chopped
1 (15-ounce) can diced tomatoes
2 (15-ounce) cans white cannellini beans

1 cup carrots, chopped
4 cups vegetable broth
1 teaspoon salt
1 (1-pound) bag baby spinach, washed

1. In a large pot over medium heat, cook the olive oil and onion for 5 minutes.
2. Add the tomatoes, beans, carrots, broth, and salt. Stir and cook for 20 minutes.
3. Add the spinach, a handful at a time, and cook for 5 minutes, until the spinach has wilted.
4. Serve warm.

Per Serving: Calories 221; Fat 6.46g; Sodium 941mg; Carbs 31.58g; Fiber 8.31g; Sugar 5.92g; Protein 10.36g

Chapter 9 Salad Recipes

- 90 Mackerel Niçoise Salad
- 90 Tahini Barley Salad
- 91 Chicken and Cabbage Salad
- 91 Green Bean Salad with Cilantro Sauce
- 92 Four-Bean Salad with Parsley and Lemon
- 92 Black-Eyed Pea and Pomegranate Salad
- 92 Sardine and Arugula Salad
- 93 Spiced Lentil and Butternut Squash Salad
- 93 Shrimp and Endive Salad
- 94 Moroccan Tomato and Roasted Pepper Salad
- 94 Mediterranean Tuna and Bean Salad
- 94 Peach and Tomato Salad
- 95 Asparagus, Arugula, and White Bean Salad
- 95 Simple Green Salad
- 95 Brussels Sprout and Kale Salad with Peanuts and Herbs
- 96 Fennel, Cherry Tomato, and Spinach Salad
- 96 Moroccan Carrot and Orange Salad
- 96 Mandarin Chicken Salad
- 97 Sesame Cucumber Salad
- 97 Za'atar Roasted Winter Squash Salad

Mackerel Niçoise Salad

Prep Time: 10 minutes | **Cook Time:** 15 minutes | **Serves:** 2

For the Dressing:
- 3 tablespoons red wine vinegar
- 4 tablespoons olive oil
- 1 teaspoon Dijon mustard
- ¼ teaspoon salt
- Pinch freshly ground black pepper

For the Salad:
- 2 teaspoons salt
- 2 small red potatoes
- 1 cup tender green beans
- 2 cups baby greens
- 2 hard-boiled eggs
- ½ cup cherry tomatoes, halved
- ⅓ cup Niçoise olives
- 2 (4-ounce) tins of mackerel fillets, drained

To make the dressing:
1. Combine the vinegar, olive oil, Dijon mustard, salt, and pepper in a lidded jar. Shake or whisk the dressing until thoroughly combined. Taste and add more salt and pepper to taste, if needed.

To make the salad:
1. Fill a large saucepan with about 3 inches of water, add salt, and bring to a boil. Add the potatoes and cook for 10 to 15 minutes, or until you can pierce them with a sharp knife, but they are still firm.
2. Remove the potatoes and add the green beans to the water. Reduce the heat and let the beans simmer for 5 minutes.
3. Place both the potatoes and green beans in a colander and run it under cold water until vegetables are cool.
4. Lay the baby greens on a large platter.
5. Slice the potatoes and arrange them on one section of the platter. Add the green beans to another section of the platter. Slice the hard-boiled eggs and arrange them in another section.
6. Continue with the tomatoes, olives, and mackerel fillets. Pour the dressing over the salad.

Per Serving: Calories 475; Fat 30.32g; Sodium 1092mg; Carbs 21.78g; Fiber 4.52g; Sugar 3.57g; Protein 29.45 g

Tahini Barley Salad

Prep Time: 15 minutes | **Cook Time:** 10 minutes | **Serves:** 4-6

- 1½ cups pearl barley
- 5 tablespoons extra-virgin olive oil, divided
- 1½ teaspoons table salt, for cooking barley
- ¼ cup tahini
- 1 teaspoon grated lemon zest plus ¼ cup juice (2 lemons)
- 1 tablespoon sumac, divided
- 1 garlic clove, minced
- ¾ teaspoon table salt
- 1 English cucumber, cut into ½-inch pieces
- 1 carrot, peeled and shredded
- 1 red bell pepper, stemmed, seeded, and chopped
- 4 scallions, sliced thin
- 2 tablespoons finely chopped jarred hot cherry peppers
- ¼ cup coarsely chopped fresh mint

1. Combine 6 cups water, barley, 1 tablespoon oil, and 1½ teaspoons salt in the Instant Pot. Lock the lid in place and close the pressure release valve. Select high pressure cook function and cook for 8 minutes. Turn off the Instant Pot and let the pressure release naturally for 15 minutes. Quick-release any remaining pressure, then carefully remove the lid, allowing the steam to escape away from you. Drain the barley, spread onto the rimmed baking sheet, and allow to cool completely, about 15 minutes.
2. Meanwhile, whisk the remaining ¼ cup oil, tahini, 2 tablespoons water, lemon zest and juice, 1 teaspoon sumac, garlic, and ¾ teaspoon salt in large bowl until combined; let sit for 15 minutes.
3. Measure out and reserve ½ cup dressing for serving. Add the barley, cucumber, carrot, bell pepper, scallions, and cherry peppers to bowl with dressing and gently toss to combine. Season with the salt and pepper to taste. Transfer the salad to a serving dish and sprinkle with the mint and remaining 2 teaspoons sumac. Serve, passing reserved dressing separately.

Per Serving: Calories 432; Fat 20.94g; Sodium 1079mg; Carbs 56.8g; Fiber 11.8g; Sugar 3.8g; Protein 9.03g

Chicken and Cabbage Salad

Prep Time: 5 minutes | **Cook Time:** 20-25 minutes | **Serves:** 6

Dressing and Chicken:
- Salt
- 1½ pounds boneless, skinless chicken breasts, trimmed of all visible fat and pounded to 1-inch thickness
- 3 tablespoons canola oil
- 1 tablespoon grated fresh ginger
- 2 garlic cloves, minced
- 5 tablespoons rice vinegar
- 2 tablespoons fish sauce
- 1–2 teaspoons Asian chili-garlic sauce

Salad:
- ½ head napa cabbage, cored and sliced thin (5½ cups)
- 2 carrots, peeled and shredded
- 4 scallions, sliced thin on bias
- ½ cup fresh cilantro leaves
- ½ cup minced fresh mint
- 3 tablespoons coarsely chopped dry-roasted unsalted peanuts

For the Dressing and Chicken:
1. Whisk 4 quarts water and 2 tablespoons salt in a Dutch oven until the salt is dissolved. Arrange the breasts, skinned side up, in the steamer basket, making sure not to overlap them. Submerge the steamer basket in water.
2. Heat a pot over medium heat, stirring the liquid occasionally to even out hot spots, until water registers 175 degrees, 15 to 20 minutes. Turn off the heat, cover the pot, remove from burner, and allow to sit until meat registers 160 degrees, 17 to 22 minutes. Transfer the chicken to paper towel–lined plate and refrigerate until cool, about 30 minutes. (Chicken can be refrigerated for up to 2 days.)
3. Pat the chicken dry with paper towels and shred into bite-size pieces with 2 forks. Heat the oil in a 12-inch skillet over medium heat until shimmering. Add the ginger and garlic and cook until fragrant, about 30 seconds. Whisk in the vinegar, fish sauce, and chili-garlic sauce and bring to simmer. Add the chicken and cook until heated through, about 1 minute.

For the Salad:
1. Combine all ingredients in a large bowl. Add the chicken mixture and gently toss to coat. Serve immediately.

Per Serving: Calories 298; Fat 13.55g; Sodium 1077mg; Carbs 10.87g; Fiber 3.2g; Sugar 4.85g; Protein 34.94g

Green Bean Salad with Cilantro Sauce

Prep Time: 5 minutes | **Cook Time:** 0 minutes | **Serves:** 8

- ¼ cup walnuts
- 2 garlic cloves, unpeeled
- 2½ cups fresh cilantro leaves and stems, trimmed (2 bunches)
- 4 teaspoons lemon juice
- 1 scallion, sliced thin
- Salt and pepper
- ½ cup extra-virgin olive oil
- 2 pounds green beans, trimmed

1. Cook the walnuts and garlic in an 8-inch skillet over medium heat, stirring often, until toasted and fragrant, 5 to 7 minutes; transfer to a bowl. Let the garlic cool slightly, then peel.
2. Process the walnuts, garlic, cilantro, lemon juice, scallion, ½ teaspoon salt, and ⅛ teaspoon pepper in a food processor until smooth, about 1 minute, scraping down sides of bowl as needed. With the processor running, slowly add the oil until incorporated; transfer to a large bowl.
3. Bring 4 quarts water to boil in a large pot. Fill the large bowl halfway with ice and water. Add the green beans and 1 tablespoon salt to boiling water and cook until crisp-tender, 3 to 5 minutes. Drain the green beans, transfer to prepared ice bath, and let sit until chilled, about 2 minutes.
4. Drain the green beans, transfer to the bowl with cilantro sauce, and gently toss to coat. (Salad can be refrigerated for up to 4 hours; bring to room temperature before serving.) Season with the pepper to taste. Serve.

Per Serving: Calories 182; Fat 16.18g; Sodium 83mg; Carbs 9.2g; Fiber 3.5g; Sugar 3.95g; Protein 2.84g

Four-Bean Salad with Parsley and Lemon

Prep Time: 20 minutes | **Cook Time:** 0 minutes | **Serves:** 4

½ cup white beans, cooked
½ cup black-eyed peas, cooked
½ cup fava beans, cooked
½ cup lima beans, cooked
1 red bell pepper, diced

1 small bunch flat-leaf parsley, chopped
2 tablespoons olive oil
1 teaspoon ground cumin
Juice of 1 lemon
Sea salt and freshly ground pepper, to taste

1. You can cook the beans a day or two in advance to speed up the preparation of this dish.
2. Combine all ingredients in a large bowl and mix well. Season to taste.
3. Allow to sit for 30 minutes, so the flavors can come together before serving.

Per Serving: Calories 165; Fat 7.5g; Sodium 200mg; Carbs 18.3g; Fiber 6.4g; Sugar 2.8g; Protein 7.2g

Black-Eyed Pea and Pomegranate Salad

Prep Time: 10 minutes | **Cook Time:** 0 minutes | **Serves:** 4

2 tablespoons extra-virgin olive oil
2 tablespoons lemon juice
2 tablespoons pomegranate molasses
¼ teaspoon ground coriander
¼ teaspoon ground cumin
⅛ teaspoon ground fennel seed

Salt and pepper
2 (15-ounce) cans no-salt-added black-eyed peas, rinsed
½ cup pomegranate seeds
½ cup minced fresh parsley
⅓ cup walnuts, toasted and chopped
4 scallions, sliced thin

1. Whisk the oil, lemon juice, pomegranate molasses, coriander, cumin, fennel seed, ¼ teaspoon salt, and ⅛ teaspoon pepper together in a large bowl until smooth. Add the peas, pomegranate seeds, parsley, walnuts, and scallions and toss to combine. Season with ⅛ teaspoon salt and pepper to taste.

Per Serving: Calories: 295; Fat: 12.89g; Sodium: 118mg; Carbs: 36.77g; Fiber: 8.92g; Sugar: 7.13g; Protein: 9.09g

Sardine and Arugula Salad

Prep Time: 20 minutes | **Cook Time:** 0 minutes | **Serves:** 6

½ cup olive oil
Juice of 1 medium lemon
1 teaspoon Dijon mustard
Sea salt and freshly ground pepper, to taste
4 medium tomatoes, diced
1 large cucumber, peeled and diced

1 pound arugula, trimmed and chopped
1 small red onion, thinly sliced
1 small bunch flat-leaf parsley, chopped
4 whole sardine fillets packed in olive oil, drained and chopped

1. For the dressing, whisk together the olive oil, lemon juice, and mustard, and season with the sea salt and pepper. Set aside.
2. In a large bowl, combine all the vegetables with the parsley, and toss. Add the sardine fillets on top of the salad.
3. Drizzle the dressing over the salad just before serving.

Per Serving: Calories 220; Fat 18.5g; Sodium 260mg; Carbs 10.6g; Fiber 2.5g; Sugar 5.3g; Protein 5.8g

Spiced Lentil and Butternut Squash Salad

Prep Time: 10 minutes | **Cook Time:** 61-86 minutes | **Serves:** 6

Salt and pepper	¼ teaspoon ground cumin
1 cup lentilles du Puy, picked over and rinsed	¼ teaspoon ground ginger
1 pound butternut squash, peeled, seeded, and cut into ½-inch pieces (3 cups)	⅛ teaspoon ground cinnamon
	1 teaspoon Dijon mustard
5 tablespoons extra-virgin olive oil	½ cup fresh parsley leaves
2 tablespoons balsamic vinegar	¼ cup finely chopped red onion
1 garlic clove, minced	1 tablespoon roasted, unsalted pepitas
½ teaspoon ground coriander	

1. Dissolve 1 teaspoon salt in 4 cups warm water (about 110 degrees) in a bowl. Add the lentils and soak at room temperature for 1 hour. Drain well.
2. Adjust the oven racks to middle and lowest positions and heat the oven to 450 degrees. Toss the squash with 1 tablespoon oil, 1½ teaspoons vinegar, ¼ teaspoon salt, and ¼ teaspoon pepper. Place the squash in a single layer on the rimmed baking sheet and roast on the lower rack until well browned and tender, 20 to 25 minutes, stirring halfway through roasting. Let cool slightly. Reduce the oven temperature to 325 degrees.
3. Cook 1 tablespoon oil, garlic, coriander, cumin, ginger, and cinnamon in a medium ovensafe saucepan over medium heat until fragrant, about 1 minute. Stir in 4 cups water and lentils. Cover, transfer the saucepan to the upper rack in the oven, and cook until lentils are tender but remain intact, 40 to 60 minutes.
4. Drain the lentils well. Whisk the remaining 3 tablespoons oil, remaining 1½ tablespoons vinegar, and mustard together in a large bowl. Add the squash, lentils, parsley, and onion and gently toss to combine. Season with the pepper to taste. Transfer to a serving platter and sprinkle with the pepitas. Serve.

Per Serving: Calories: 248; Fat: 12.2g; Sodium: 35mg; Carbs: 28.87g; Fiber: 6.1g; Sugar: 4.87g; Protein: 5.13g

Shrimp and Endive Salad

Prep Time: 15 minutes | **Cook Time:** 2 minutes | **Serves:** 4

¼ cup olive oil	2 cups salted water
1 small shallot, minced	14 shrimp, peeled and deveined
1 tablespoon Dijon mustard	1 head endive
Juice and zest of 1 lemon	½ cup tart green apple, diced
Sea salt and freshly ground pepper, to taste	2 tablespoons toasted walnuts

1. For the vinaigrette, whisk together the first five ingredients in a small bowl until creamy and emulsified.
2. Refrigerate for at least 2 hours for best flavor.
3. In a small pan, boil salted water. Add the shrimp and cook for 1–2 minutes, or until the shrimp turns pink. Drain and cool under cold water.
4. To assemble the salad, wash and break the endive. Place on serving plates and top with the shrimp, green apple, and toasted walnuts.
5. Drizzle with the vinaigrette before serving.

Per Serving: Calories 210; Fat 15g; Sodium 420mg; Carbs 10.2g; Fiber 2.1g; Sugar 5.6g; Protein 10.8g

Moroccan Tomato and Roasted Pepper Salad

Prep Time: 15 minutes | **Cook Time:** 0 minutes | **Serves:** 6

2 large green bell peppers	4 tablespoons olive oil
1 hot red chili Fresno or jalapeño pepper	1 teaspoon ground cumin
4 large tomatoes, peeled, seeded, and diced	Juice of 1 lemon
1 large cucumber, peeled and diced	Sea salt and freshly ground pepper, to taste
1 small bunch flat-leaf parsley, chopped	

1. Preheat the broiler on high. Broil all of the peppers and chilies until the skin blackens and blisters.
2. Place the peppers and chilies in a paper bag. Seal and set aside to cool. Combine the rest of the ingredients in a medium bowl and mix well.
3. Take peppers and chilies out from the bag and remove the skins. Seed and chop the peppers and add them to the salad.
4. Season with the sea salt and freshly ground pepper.
5. Toss to combine and let sit for 15–20 minutes before serving.

Per Serving: Calories 110; Fat 7.5g; Sodium 170mg; Carbs 11.2g; Fiber 3.4g; Sugar 6.7g; Protein 1.8g

Mediterranean Tuna and Bean Salad

Prep Time: 15 minutes | **Cook Time:** 0 minutes | **Serves:** 4

¼ cup olive oil	4–6 cups baby greens
¼ cup balsamic vinegar	1 (6-ounce) can solid white albacore tuna, drained
½ teaspoon minced garlic	1 cup canned garbanzo beans, rinsed and drained
¼ teaspoon dried oregano	¼ cup low-salt olives, pitted and quartered
Sea salt and freshly ground pepper, to taste	2 Roma tomatoes, chopped
2 tablespoons capers, drained	

1. To make the vinaigrette, whisk together the olive oil, balsamic vinegar, garlic, oregano, sea salt, and pepper until emulsified.
2. Stir in the capers. Refrigerate for up to 6 hours before serving.
3. Place the baby greens in a salad bowl or on individual plates, and top with the tuna, beans, olives, and tomatoes.
4. Drizzle the vinaigrette over all, and serve immediately.

Per Serving: Calories 261; Fat 18.34g; Sodium 506mg; Carbs 11.68g; Fiber 3.7g; Sugar 4.77g; Protein 13.37g

Peach and Tomato Salad

Prep Time: 15 minutes | **Cook Time:** 0 minutes | **Serves:** 2

2 ripe peaches, pitted and sliced into wedges	Sea salt and freshly ground pepper, to taste
2 ripe tomatoes, cut into wedges	3 tablespoons olive oil
½ red onion, thinly sliced	1 tablespoon lemon juice

1. Toss the peaches, tomatoes, and red onion in a large bowl. Season to taste.
2. Add the olive oil and lemon juice, and gently toss. Serve at room temperature.

Per Serving: Calories 273; Fat 20.93g; Sodium 298mg; Carbs 22.38g; Fiber 4.3g; Sugar 17.18g; Protein 2.81g

Asparagus, Arugula, and White Bean Salad

Prep Time: 5 minutes | Cook Time: 5 minutes | Serves: 6

5 tablespoons extra-virgin olive oil	Salt and pepper
½ red onion, sliced thin	1 (15-ounce) can no-salt-added cannellini beans, rinsed
1 pound asparagus, trimmed and cut into 1-inch lengths on bias	2 tablespoons plus 2 teaspoons balsamic vinegar
	6 ounces (6 cups) baby arugula

1. Heat 2 tablespoons oil in a 12-inch nonstick skillet over high heat until just smoking. Add the onion and cook until lightly browned, about 1 minute. Add the asparagus, ¼ teaspoon pepper, and ¼ teaspoon salt and cook, stirring occasionally, until the asparagus is browned and crisp-tender, about 4 minutes. Transfer to a bowl, stir in the beans, and let cool slightly.
2. Whisk the remaining 3 tablespoons oil, ¼ teaspoon salt, vinegar, and ⅛ teaspoon pepper together in a small bowl. Gently toss the arugula with 2 tablespoons dressing until coated. Season with the pepper to taste. Divide the arugula among individual plates. Gently toss the asparagus mixture with the remaining dressing and arrange over the arugula. Serve.

Per Serving: Calories 174; Fat 11.74g; Sodium 464mg; Carbs 13.85g; Fiber 4.6g; Sugar 2.96g; Protein 5.31g

Simple Green Salad

Prep Time: 10 minutes | Cook Time: 0 minutes | Serves: 4

½ garlic clove, peeled	⅛ teaspoon pepper
3 tablespoons extra-virgin olive oil	8 ounces (8 cups) green leaf lettuce, torn into bite-size pieces if necessary
2 tablespoons vinegar	
¼ teaspoon salt	

1. Rub inside of salad bowl with the garlic. Whisk the oil, salt, vinegar, and pepper in the bowl until combined. Add lettuce and gently toss to coat. Serve.

Per Serving: Calories 103; Fat 10.24g; Sodium 166mg; Carbs 2.31g; Fiber 1g; Sugar 0.6g; Protein 1.01g

Brussels Sprout and Kale Salad with Peanuts and Herbs

Prep Time: 5 minutes | Cook Time: 0 minutes | Serves: 4

⅓ cup cider vinegar	thin
2 tablespoons extra-virgin olive oil	8 ounces Tuscan kale, stemmed and sliced into ¼-inch-wide strips (4½ cups)
1 tablespoon lime juice	
½ teaspoon ground coriander	¼ cup dry-roasted, unsalted peanuts, chopped
Salt and pepper	1 tablespoon chopped fresh cilantro
1 pound Brussels sprouts, trimmed, halved, and sliced very	1 tablespoon chopped fresh mint

1. Whisk the vinegar, oil, lime juice, coriander, ¼ teaspoon pepper, and ¼ teaspoon salt together in a large bowl. Add the Brussels sprouts and gently toss to coat. Cover and let sit for at least 30 minutes or up to 2 hours.
2. Vigorously squeeze and massage the kale with hands until leaves are uniformly darkened and slightly wilted, about 1 minute. Add the kale, peanuts, cilantro, and mint to the bowl with Brussels sprouts and gently toss to coat. Season with the pepper to taste. Serve.

Per Serving: Calories 194; Fat 12.16g; Sodium 198mg; Carbs 17.37g; Fiber 7.3g; Sugar 4.35g; Protein 8.69g

Fennel, Cherry Tomato, and Spinach Salad

Prep Time: 15 minutes | **Cook Time:** 0 minutes | **Serves:** 2

4 tablespoons chicken broth	1 fennel bulb, sliced
4 cups baby spinach leaves	¼ cup olive oil
10 cherry tomatoes, halved	Juice of 2 lemons
Sea salt and freshly ground pepper, to taste	

1. In a large sauté pan, heat the chicken broth over medium heat. Add the spinach and tomatoes and cook until spinach is wilted. Season with the salt and pepper to taste.
2. Remove from heat and toss fennel slices in with the spinach and tomatoes. Let the fennel warm in the pan, then transfer to a large bowl.
3. Drizzle with the olive oil and lemon juice, and serve immediately.

Per Serving: Calories 317; Fat 27.83g; Sodium 520mg; Carbs 17.67g; Fiber 6.2g; Sugar 8.43g; Protein 4.31g

Moroccan Carrot and Orange Salad

Prep Time: 5 minutes | **Cook Time:** 0 minutes | **Serves:** 6

2 oranges	Salt and pepper
1 tablespoon lemon juice	1 pound carrots, peeled and shredded
¾ teaspoon ground cumin	3 tablespoons minced fresh cilantro
⅛ teaspoon cayenne pepper	3 tablespoons extra-virgin olive oil
⅛ teaspoon ground cinnamon	

1. Cut off the peel and pith of oranges. Holding fruit over bowl, use a paring knife to slice between membranes to release segments. Cut the segments in half crosswise and let drain in a fine-mesh strainer set over a large bowl, reserving the juice.
2. Whisk lemon juice, cumin, cayenne, cinnamon, and ½ teaspoon salt into bowl with reserved orange juice. Add orange segments and carrots and gently toss to coat. Let sit until liquid starts to pool in bottom of bowl, 3 to 5 minutes.
3. Drain salad in fine-mesh strainer then return to bowl. (Salad can be refrigerated for up to 1 hour; bring to room temperature before serving.) Stir in cilantro and oil and season with pepper to taste. Serve.

Per Serving: Calories 114; Fat 7.11g; Sodium 150mg; Carbs 13.1g; Fiber 3.4g; Sugar 7.96g; Protein 1.12g

Mandarin Chicken Salad

Prep Time: 20 minutes | **Cook Time:** 0 minutes | **Serves:** 6

3 cups cut-up cooked chicken	1 can (8 oz) sliced water chestnuts, drained
¾ cup sliced green grapes	1 container (6 oz) lemon fat-free yogurt
2 medium stalks celery, thinly sliced (1 cup)	2 tablespoons reduced-sodium soy sauce
2 green onions, thinly sliced	Mixed salad greens
1 can (11 oz) mandarin orange segments, drained	

1. In a large bowl, mix the chicken, grapes, celery, onions, orange segments and water chestnuts. In a small bowl, mix the yogurt and soy sauce. Pour over the chicken mixture; toss until combined.
2. Cover and refrigerate at least 2 hours or until chilled. Serve on the salad greens.

Per Serving: Calories 210; Fat 3.95g; Sodium 320mg; Carbs 20.65g; Fiber 2.1g; Sugar 14.35g; Protein 23.5g

Sesame Cucumber Salad

Prep Time: 5 minutes | **Cook Time:** 0 minutes | **Serves:** 4

3 cucumbers, peeled, halved lengthwise, seeded, and sliced ¼ inch thick	2 tablespoons toasted sesame oil
Salt and pepper	1 tablespoon lemon juice
¼ cup rice vinegar	1 tablespoon sesame seeds, toasted
	⅛ teaspoon red pepper flakes, plus extra for seasoning

1. Toss the cucumbers with 1 tablespoon salt in a colander set over a large bowl. Weight the cucumbers with 1 gallon-size zipper-lock bag filled with water; drain for 1 to 3 hours. Rinse and pat dry.
2. Whisk the vinegar, oil, lemon juice, sesame seeds, and pepper flakes together in a large bowl. Add the cucumbers and gently toss to coat. Season with the pepper to taste. Serve at room temperature or chilled.

Per Serving: Calories 95; Fat 8.29g; Sodium 150mg; Carbs 4.02g; Fiber 1.4g; Sugar 2.25g; Protein 1.33g

Za'atar Roasted Winter Squash Salad

Prep Time: 5 minutes | **Cook Time:** 20-35 minutes | **Serves:** 6

3 pounds butternut squash, peeled, seeded, and cut into ½-inch pieces (8 cups)	1 small shallot, minced
¼ cup extra-virgin olive oil	2 tablespoons lemon juice
Salt and pepper	¾ cup fresh parsley leaves
1½ teaspoons za'atar	⅓ cup roasted unsalted pepitas
	½ cup pomegranate seeds

1. Adjust the oven rack to lowest position and heat the oven to 450 degrees. Toss the squash with 1 tablespoon oil and season with the pepper. Arrange the squash in a single layer on the rimmed baking sheet and roast until well browned and tender, 30 to 35 minutes, stirring halfway through roasting. Sprinkle the squash with za'atar and let cool for 15 minutes. (Squash can be refrigerated for up to 24 hours; bring to room temperature before continuing.)
2. Whisk the shallot, lemon juice, ¼ teaspoon salt, and remaining 3 tablespoons oil together in a large bowl. Add the squash, parsley, and pepitas and gently toss to coat. Sprinkle with the pomegranate seeds. Serve.

Per Serving: Calories 236; Fat 12.65g; Sodium 15mg; Carbs 31.35g; Fiber 5.9g; Sugar 7.38g; Protein 4.74g

Conclusion

The best time to take control of your health is right now. With The Ultimate Zero Point Weight Loss Cookbook, you've gained not just a collection of recipes, but a powerful tool to transform your lifestyle. Each recipe has been crafted to provide nourishing, delicious meals that keep you feeling full, energized, and confident in your weight-loss journey. Zero point foods allow you to focus on what truly matters—building sustainable habits that support your long-term goals.

The beauty of this cookbook lies in its versatility. Whether you're cooking for yourself, your family, or entertaining guests, you now have a wealth of recipes that suit any occasion without compromising your health objectives. From quick and easy weekday meals to special dishes for celebrations, you can approach every meal with excitement and confidence.

As you continue this journey, remember that small, consistent steps lead to lasting change. Keep your kitchen stocked with fresh, Zero point ingredients, and don't be afraid to explore new flavors or put your own twist on the recipes. Cooking is a creative process, and the more you experiment, the more you'll discover what works best for you.

So, take charge, embrace the joy of cooking, and let your kitchen become a space of empowerment and transformation. Each recipe is an opportunity to nourish not only your body but also your spirit. Your goals are within reach, and every meal brings you closer to the healthy, vibrant life you deserve. Start now, explore the possibilities, and let The Ultimate Zero Point Weight Loss Cookbook guide you on your path to success. Your next great dish awaits—get cooking today!

Appendix 1 Measurement Conversion Chart

VOLUME EQUIVALENTS (LIQUID)

US STANDARD	US STANDARD (OUNCES)	METRIC (APPROXIMATE)
2 tablespoons	1 fl.oz	30 mL
¼ cup	2 fl.oz	60 mL
½ cup	4 fl.oz	120 mL
1 cup	8 fl.oz	240 mL
1½ cup	12 fl.oz	355 mL
2 cups or 1 pint	16 fl.oz	475 mL
4 cups or 1 quart	32 fl.oz	1 L
1 gallon	128 fl.oz	4 L

VOLUME EQUIVALENTS (DRY)

US STANDARD	METRIC (APPROXIMATE)
⅛ teaspoon	0.5 mL
¼ teaspoon	1 mL
½ teaspoon	2 mL
¾ teaspoon	4 mL
1 teaspoon	5 mL
1 tablespoon	15 mL
¼ cup	59 mL
½ cup	118 mL
¾ cup	177 mL
1 cup	235 mL
2 cups	475 mL
3 cups	700 mL
4 cups	1 L

TEMPERATURES EQUIVALENTS

FAHRENHEIT(F)	CELSIUS(C) (APPROXIMATE)
225 °F	107 °C
250 °F	120 °C
275 °F	135 °C
300 °F	150 °C
325 °F	160 °C
350 °F	180 °C
375 °F	190 °C
400 °F	205 °C
425 °F	220 °C
450 °F	235 °C
475 °F	245 °C
500 °F	260 °C

WEIGHT EQUIVALENTS

US STANDARD	METRIC (APPROXINATE)
1 ounce	28 g
2 ounces	57 g
5 ounces	142 g
10 ounces	284 g
15 ounces	425 g
16 ounces (1 pound)	455 g
1.5 pounds	680 g
2 pounds	907 g

Appendix 2 Recipes Index

A
Air Fryer Herbed Tuna Steaks 80
Air Fryer Popcorn 52
Air Fryer Roasted Radishes 37
Air-Fried Garlic Dill Beets 39
Asparagus, Arugula, and White Bean Salad 95
Authentic Moussaka 34

B
Baked Brown Rice with Mushrooms and Edamame 44
Baked Cod with Lemon-Caper Sauce 76
Baked Salmon and Cherry Tomato Pockets 80
Balsamic Rosemary Pork Tenderloin 68
Beef Osso Buco 66
Black-Eyed Pea and Pomegranate Salad 92
Blackberry Quinoa Bowl 26
Blueberry Chia Oatmeal 29
Blueberry Power Breakfast Smoothie 32
Braised Beef Brisket with Onions 67
Braised Chicken with Chickpeas and Chermoula 60
Braised Lamb Shanks in Herbed Tomato Sauce 66
Brown Rice with Apricots, Cherries, and Pecans 42
Brussels Sprout and Kale Salad with Peanuts and Herbs 95
Buckwheat and Root Vegetable Bake 45

C
Caramelized Onion Lentil and Rice Bowl 43
Cherry Barbecue Chicken Cutlets 58
Chicken and Cabbage Salad 91
Chicken Shawarma with Chickpeas and Sweet Potato 57
Chilled Cucumber Soup 83
Citrus Swordfish with Fresh Herbs 78
Cottage Cheese Breakfast Bowl 27
Crispy Herbed White Beans 51
Crunchy Turmeric Chickpeas 50
Cucumber and Tomato Salad with Egg Whites 31
Curried Zucchini and Apple Soup 88

D
Deviled Eggs with Yogurt and Dill 51
Dukkah-Spiced Cod with Beet and Arugula Salad 79

E
Eggplant Egg Breakfast Sandwich 28

F
Fennel, Cherry Tomato, and Spinach Salad 96
Four-Bean Salad with Parsley and Lemon 92
Fried Eggs and Lettuce 32

G
Garlic Herb Roasted Grape Tomatoes 38
Garlic Roasted Brussels Sprouts with Orange 35
Garlic Roasted Tomatoes and Olives 52
Garlic Roasted Zucchini with Pepper 39
Garlic-Balsamic Shrimp 80
Garlicky Sautéed Greens 37
Garlicky Swiss Chard with Fried Eggs 26
Greek Baked Butter Beans 42
Greek Roasted Vegetables 36
Greek Turkey and Rice Skillet 63
Greek Yogurt and Berry Bowl 32
Greek-Style Lamb Chops 65
Green Bean Salad with Cilantro Sauce 91
Grilled Chicken and Vegetables with Lemon-Walnut Sauce 63
Grilled Greek-Inspired Beef Kebabs 72
Grilled Halibut with Romesco Sauce 77
Grilled Lemon Herb Chicken Breasts 57
Grilled Lemon-Garlic Salmon 75
Grilled Spiced Pork Tenderloin 66

H
Hearty Paella Soup 84
Herb-Marinated Grilled Flank Steak 68
Herbed Barley Pilaf with Mushrooms and Almonds 47
Herbed Garlic Popcorn 54
Herbed Scrambled Eggs 31
Homemade Chicken Shawarma 59
Homemade Refried Beans 42
Homemade Vegetable Fagioli 84
Huevos Rancheros 30

I
Instant Pot Provençal Chicken Soup 86
Italian Roasted Vegetables 35
Italian Turkey Meatballs and Zoodles 57

K
Kofta with Vegetables in Tomato Sauce 71

L
Lebanese Grilled Chicken 59
Lemon and Thyme Roasted Vegetables 34
Lemon Baked Halibut with Cherry Tomatoes 81
Lemon Chicken Soup 85
Lemon Garlic Chicken Thighs 63
Lemon Garlic Hummus 51

Lemon Garlic Shrimp 49
Lemon Herb-Crusted Pork Tenderloin 70
Lemon Herbed Chicken 61
Lemon-Garlic Roasted Trout 78
Lemony Bulgur with Kale and Tomatoes 43
Lemony Green Beans with Red Onions 38
Lemony Quinoa with Broccoli and Potatoes 43
Lemony White Bean and Kale Soup 88
Lentils with Spinach and Crispy Garlic 46

M

Mackerel Niçoise Salad 90
Mandarin Chicken Salad 96
Marinated Mushrooms and Olives 50
Mediterranean Baked Salmon with Tomatoes and Olives 76
Mediterranean Beef Stew 87
Mediterranean Pork Chops with Olives 69
Mediterranean Slow-Cooked Turkey Breast 60
Mediterranean Tuna and Bean Salad 94
Moroccan Carrot and Orange Salad 96
Moroccan Chicken and Vegetable Tagine 62
Moroccan Lamb Shanks and Potatoes 72
Moroccan Lentil Soup 86
Moroccan Rice and Chickpea Bake 41
Moroccan Seafood Stew 85
Moroccan Tomato and Roasted Pepper Salad 94
Moroccan-Spiced Chicken with Saffron Rice 62
Moroccan-Spiced Sea Bass 77
Mushroom Barley Pilaf 44

O

Oatmeal with Apples and Cinnamon 27
Orange Chicken with Pecan Wild Rice 59
Oven Roasted Cauliflower with Lemon Tahini Sauce 36

P

Pan-Seared Sea Bass 81
Peach and Tomato Salad 94
Poached Chicken Breasts with Tomato-Ginger Vinaigrette 56
Pork and Cannellini Bean Stew 83
Pumpkin Rice Patties 53

R

Raspberry Banana Smoothie 27
Roasted Chicken Breasts with Ratatouille 56
Roasted Chicken with Tzatziki Sauce 61
Roasted Cod with Olives and Artichokes 78
Roasted Grape Tomatoes and Asparagus 35
Roasted Herbed Beef Tips 65
Roasted Pork Tenderloin with Chermoula Sauce 65
Roasted Pork Tenderloin with Cherry-Balsamic Sauce 70
Roasted Red Pepper Tapenade 52
Roasted Sea Bass with Root Vegetables 76
Roasted Spiced Chickpeas 49
Roasted Whole Red Snapper with Dill 75
Rosemary Roasted Red Potatoes 38

S

Sardine and Arugula Salad 92
Scrambled Eggs with Arugula and Radish Salad 28
Seared Scallops with Rosemary White Bean Purée 74
Sesame Cucumber Salad 97
Shredded Chicken Souvlaki 61
Shrimp and Endive Salad 93
Sicilian Escarole and White Beans 46
Simple Green Salad 95
Slow Cooker Italian Beef Ragù 67
Slow Cooker Ratatouille 39
Slow Cooker Vegan Bean Chili 47
Slow-Cooked Herbed Leg of Lamb 68
Slow-Cooked Kofta Casserole 58
Slow-Cooked Moroccan Lamb Roast 71
Spiced Lentil and Butternut Squash Salad 93
Spiced Red Lentils 41
Spiced Roasted Cashews 54
Spiced Roasted Mini Potatoes 37
Spicy Barbecued Scallops and Shrimp 74
Spinach and Mushroom Omelet 27
Spinach Stuffed Flank Steak 69
Steamed Cod with Swiss Chard 79
Steamed Lemon Salmon 75
Strawberry Spinach Avocado Smoothie 26
Stuffed Cucumber Cups 53
Stuffed Pepper Stew 87
Sweet Potato Chips 50

T

Tahini Barley Salad 90
Thyme Grilled Pork Chops 67
Tofu Scramble and Roasted Potatoes 30
Turkish Spiced Mixed Nuts 53
Tuscan White Beans with Rosemary and Sage 45

V

Vegan Tofu Scramble 29
Vegetable Scramble 31

W

White Bean and Vegetable Soup 83
White Bean Stew 88

Z

Za'atar Roasted Winter Squash Salad 97
Zucchini and Bell Pepper Frittata 29

Made in the USA
Las Vegas, NV
10 March 2025